8/6

OXFORD
(Christminster)

WANTAGE
(Alfredstone)

• FAWLEY MAGNA
(Marygreen)

WINDSOR
(Castle Royal)

NEWBURY
(Kennetbridge)

READING
(Aldbrickham)

ĿTSHIRE
(MID WESSEX)

BASINGSTOKE
(Stoke Barehills)

HAMPSHIRE
(Upper Wessex)

ALDERSHOT
(Quartershot)

ĿE GREAT
PLAIN

WEYHILL
(Weydon Priors)

ĿNEHENGE

SALISBURY
(Melchester)

WINCHESTER
(Wintoncester)

ĿBURY

SOUTHAMPTON

ĿTRIDGE
(Trantridge)

ĿTER CRANBOURNE
NEWTON (Chaseborough)

FORD

HORTON INN
(Lew ton Inn)

WIMBORNE

NEW
FOREST

MELSIER (Warborne)

HARBOROUGH PARK

DOLE (Hintock/Kingsbere House)

BOURNEMOUTH
(Sandbourne)

ĿFE

ĿWANAGE
(Knollsea)

ISLE OF
WIGHT

ĿLAND

THOMAS HARDY'S
WESSEX SCENE

First Impression, April 1948.
Second Impression, June 1957.
Third Impression, March 1968.

THOMAS HARDY'S
WESSEX SCENE

By

CLIVE HOLLAND

Author of " Wessex," "Thomas Hardy, O.M.
The Man, His Works and the Land of Wessex,"
&c., &c.

With Frontispiece and 18 Illustrations
from Original Drawings
by Douglas Snowdon.

DORCHESTER :
Printed and Published by Longmans (Dorchester) Ltd.
The Friary Press, Dorchester, Dorset, England.

PREFACE

By some strange chance, in the passage of years, the term Wessex, as standing for that portion of Southern and South-Western England, which in Saxon times formed the Kingdom of the West Saxons, almost passed out of the language, and lost significance other than as a mere historical term. It had, of course, long ceased to appear on ordinary maps.

Indeed, it was left to the genius of Thomas Hardy, Wessex-born poet and novelist, to revive the name, three-quarters of a century ago. And by such a re-incarnation to create a keen, and increasing interest in the district that he made his own in Literature, as regards its people, characteristics and beauty,

The Wessex of Thomas Hardy is, of course, Dorset: with the exception of a few places mentioned by him in neighbouring counties. It presents to those who visit it a variety of life, character, picturesque scenery, and historical and archæological survivals that cannot fail to interest and charm. This portion, indeed, of England of which Hardy has left so valuable a record of things that have and are passing so swiftly away in what, perhaps, is incorrectly described as 'the march of modern progress,' invites attention and study like some beautiful low toned picture.

In the present book an attempt has been made to present the personality of Hardy, as sensed by the writer during a long friendship and knowledge of him ; and also to provide a guide to many of the beauty spots, interesting towns and picturesque villages he described in his novels and poems.

Within the scope of a volume such as the present, it has been obviously impossible to include all which one wished to do. I hope, however that my book may bring a new picture of Hardy, the man, to many readers ; and also induce many to visit " Hardy's Wessex Scene," and thus get to know a fascinatingly interesting portion of England.

CLIVE HOLLAND.

March, 1948.

CONTENTS

ILLUSTRATIONS

CHAPTER I

THE MAN HE WAS AND BECAME

I T IS MORE YEARS THAN, perhaps, one likes to remember since I received my first letter from Thomas Hardy, and, next day, on his invitation, knocked on the door of " Max Gate," his home just outside Dorchester. I had cycled over from Bournemouth, where I then lived, on a beautiful morning in July. I had come through Wareham, the Anglebury of *The Hand of Ethelberta*, and *The Return of the Native*, along the valley of the Frome, with its meads, and the sparkling little river glinting in the sunshine.

And then on my way through a stretch of country, that brought to mind both *Tess of the D'Urbervilles* and *Far from the Madding Crowd*, the former of which had not long been published and I had been reading. " Max Gate " was not then as enshrouded by trees from the road as it afterwards became. Indeed, it had fine views from its upper windows. I was shown into the sunny drawingroom with its many pictures, some of them etchings, and others watercolours of scenes and places in Hardy's novels. Also cabinets containing china, and others of the many things ; Roman pottery, glass and metal ornaments, that had been dug up on the site, when the foundations of the house were being prepared.

Dorchester, when Cæsar's legions were in Britain, was an important Roman station which was named Durnovaria, and many relics of the occupation are from time to time found. And while I was waiting for Hardy's appearance I examined those in the cabinets.

He came into the room smiling ; and, setting me at my ease, we were soon chatting animatedly.

He rather surprised me, for he did not look at all like the accepted idea of a distinguished author ; or, indeed, of an author at all. Of middle height, with a rather heavy moustache, he was wearing a by no means smart suit of a brownish-grey tweed, with loose knickerbockers buckled in just below the knees, and dark grey stockings.

I had told him, when writing to him, sometime before my visit, that I had been commissioned to write a book about Wessex, which was to be illustrated with a large number of coloured reproductions of watercolours to be painted by a well-known artist, Walter Tyndale, who was coming down to spend a summer holiday engaged on the work.

Hardy was much interested, and, if I remember rightly, on several occasions, he had seen and admired Walter Tyndale's work. And, as I afterwards discovered, anything that would make his native county better known pleased him.

He quite eagerly discussed the proposed scope of the book, and gave me some valuable hints as to localities that should be illustrated and described.

On the same day I met the first Mrs. Hardy at lunch. She was a handsome woman, hospitable and kindly ; the owner all her life of some beautiful cats, of which she was very proud, and concerning which she wrote verses, which were occasionally published in the " Dorset County Chronicle."

" Max Gate," which Hardy himself had designed, struck me as a very comfortable and convenient house, and in several respects, as regarded the latter characteristic, somewhat in advance of the times. His study, or rather the first, for in all he had three, was a large and pleasant room on the first floor lined with books, and with a charming view of the garden. It was in this room that I later on took several photos of him in surroundings that best befit a literary man.

Thus began a friendship that lasted for many years, and afforded me a knowledge of the man, his habits, thoughts, ambitions and charm, that is an ineffaceable and treasured memory.

Thomas Hardy's Birthplace. Upper Bockhampton.

Douglas Sharpor

Those who know Hardy's ancestry and the circumstances of birth and parentage, also his environment from boyhood might say " Surely the ' little folk,' those legendary ' pixies,' must have been at hand when he was born."

It was in a thatched cottage-like dwelling of rather unusual size, that on June 2nd, 1840 Thomas Hardy came into the world. His birthplace stands at Upper Bockhampton just below the outskirts of Egdon Heath, a mile or two from Dorchester. We are told that he was a frail baby who, at his birth, but for the intelligence and prompt action of the village midwife would never have survived.

The attendant doctor thought that the baby was dead, and placed him in a basket as being so. The woman was, however, not satisfied. She lifted the baby out of the basket, and took such measures as would be likely to awaken any life that might flicker in him. It was her skill, foresight and persistence, that saved for English literature a baby who was destined to become famous as a great novelist and also as a poet of the mid-Victorian Era.

Even today Upper Bockhampton is a little ' off the map.' At the time of Hardy's birth one had to leave the main road into Dorchester to reach the cottage, the few other dwellings and the Inn, and approach the hamlet along the ancient Roman highway, of which Hardy wrote under the title of " The Roman Road " in his volume of poems *Time's Laughing Stocks*.

Here is his vivid description :—

" The Roman road runs straight and bare,
 As pale parting-line in hair,
 Across the heath. And thoughtful men,
 Contrast its days of Now, and Then,
 And delve and measure and compare.
 Visioning on the vacant air
 Helmed legionaries, who proudly rear
 The eagle, and they pace again
 The Roman Road."

His native village was, indeed, a place remote from the life of the nation. And the wide stretch of heath, within a short distance of his home, known as Bockhampton Heath, which joined Puddletown Heath, and to which Hardy gave the name " Egdon," undoubtedly exercised a remarkable influence on him from his earliest years. We know that from a small child onwards he frequented it, studied it and dreamed of it.

Hardy's home today remains, fortunately, very much as he knew it, and as when he was born. It was one of the larger houses of the village.

The Heath gloomy and grim, except in Spring and Summer, when its vastness, purple heather, and golden gorse renders it beautiful and impressive, was, indeed, the dominating Nature influence of his early life. Indeed, it figures in his novels and poems far more frequently than any other single natural feature or district. And those who believe in the influence of environment, as well as intellectural influences, in the fashioning of character have little difficulty in tracing some of Hardy's fatalistic outlook upon life to the influence of this stretch of moorland.

From all that I was able to ascertain from those who knew his mother, and from what has been written concerning her, Mrs. Hardy had the conventionally religious mind of those days. She was known as what was described as a " good woman," and she was certainly, from all accounts, a good mother. And undoubtedly brought up her son to religious observances. The family attended Stinsford Church, in the graveyard of which, at his request, Hardy's heart now lies buried. And the choir and musicians of the church when Hardy was a boy, used to practice the tunes for Sunday services in the kitchen of his home. It was an instrumental choir, as well as vocal. On these occasions his fondness for music was acquired.

As the Mellstock Quire, the performers appear in several of his poems notably in *The Dead Quire* and *The Noble Lady's Tale.*

Occasionally Mrs. Hardy and her children, including Thomas, went into Dorchester to St. Peter's, the principal Church, which stands at the junction of Cornhill and High East Street and High West Street. In fact there is evidence that the Hardy family for several generations were known as lovers of music, and it was an inherited characteristic with Thomas Hardy. His father before him was especially interested in music. Hardy's grandfather, as a young man, used to play the 'cello in the choir at Puddletown (Weatherbury) Church, where the Jacobean gallery, in which he sat with his companions, is still to be seen. An interesting survival in the church at which, in *Far from the Madding Crowd*, Gabriel Oak and Bathsheba Everdene were married.

Some writers have sought to trace Hardy's descent from the branch of the family to which Nelson's Hardy, the Captain of the ' Victory ' belonged. He undoubtedly came of the Dorset Hardy's branch, but Hardy never made any claim to kinship with Captain Hardy.

In the drawingroom at " Max Gate " on one occasion, when I had asked him a question regarding this possible kinship, he shook his head in dissent.

Afterwards he showed me an elaborate genealogical ' tree ' ; going back several generations, which he had, I understood, himself prepared. But there was no showing on it of the branch leading down from the historic Naval Captain Hardy.

Hardy's father was a builder, and at one time the employer of a considerable number of work-people, and, in Hardy's youth, was accounted a prosperous man. And, from this fact, one can trace the circumstances which led to his son entering the profession of an architect. His position enabled his father to occupy a certain social standing in the village, and doubtless allowed him to make his quite considerable house a gathering place for the local musicians, who not only practised the church music for Sundays, but also that of dances, and rounds for any village jollifications which took place.

The social events which were held at his father's house made their lasting impression upon Hardy's mind. He doubtless delighted in the scraping of the fiddles, booming of the bass viols, shrill notes of the flutes, and softer ones of the clarionets. Lingering memories of these evening practices are found in his novels, tales and poetry.

These happenings and his association with his father's workmen, the maids that the Hardys were in a position to employ, and the farm labourers with whom he was brought in contact made deep impressions upon the child's mind and that of early boyhood.

No one, I think, who was brought into close contact with Hardy in later years, and knew him and talked with him, could fail to remark on his extraordinarily vivid memory of scenes he had witnessed in childhood. Many of which recollections, in the case of an ordinary child, would certainly have faded.

Hardy's early life affords, indeed, a very fascinating field of speculation. His mother was undoubtedly an exceptional woman of some very considerable gifts of character. And she had a distinctly educative influence upon her son, whose home life, probably largely due to her, was lifted to a higher plane than that of outside influences arising from his association with the rougher and more elemental life that was led in those days by the majority of villagers and their children.

Indeed many critics of his work as a novelist, and those who knew him personally and wrote of him, have referred to a conflict as of two distinct personalities, and those who conversed with him could not, I think, have failed to detect this characteristic, which often caused him to appear to retire suddenly into himself, after an instance of unusual confidence.

I remember an old inhabitant of Dorchester, Hardy's senior by some years, who died only a short time before Hardy himself passed away, told how Hardy in early life, was shy and very retiring, which led to his being considered, by the boys and girls with whom he associated, as " stuck up " and even " queer." This opinion of him arose undoubtedly from his being introspective, and of a lonely disposition ; preferring isolation rather than companionship.

It sets no great problem for a psychologist to estimate the ultimate influence of this, and also that of spiritual and intellectual isolation, upon his later character and achievements.

In fact almost anyone who has read his novels and poems carefully can easily realise a picture of his childhood ; his surroundings ; his early friends in the village ; and the nature of his associations with the older people of the little Wessex hamlet where he lived. All these things had a very material influence upon a mind which in later years developed a mental and analytical detachment regarding the peasantry of his native county, which did not, however, prevent his having a very sympathetic appreciation of their struggles, vicissitudes and mental processes that are so clearly demonstrated in his writings.

That his mother was a woman of considerable natural culture cannot well be doubted. And he owed her much as regards her care of him, encouragement to study and to read what are usually described as " good " and instructive books. She even procured for him copies of the classics. And her influence led him to set his ambition towards social advancement, rather than to identify himself too closely with his surroundings and peasant associates.

Hardy was proud of his ancestry which was traceable from a French family named Le Hardi, of influence and distinction, that originally had settled in the island of Jersey. A son of whom, named John, in the 16th century emigrated to England and eventually settled, it is thought, with his wife and children in the valley of the Frome not far from Dorchester. This event may be taken to fix the connection of the Le Hardi's with the later spelling of the ' Hardy ' family in Dorsetshire.

Another fact in connection with this settlement is that at the end of the 16th century and onwards, the name " Thomas " became a very frequent one in the family. One of whom, living at Melcombe Regis near Weymouth, became a benefactor to Dorchester by leaving in his will an annual sum of fifty pounds for charitable purposes : and in 1569 founded the Grammar School in South Street which bears his name.

The foregoing account of the Le Hardi family's ancestors serves to link up that of the famous novelist and poet with an ancestry of which I know, from what he himself told me, he was very proud. An interesting fact is that there was, centuries ago, a poet in the Le Hardi family of some distinction.

Little is known regarding Hardy's education in the usual acceptance of the word, until he became a pupil at a private school, the master of which, a Mr. Isaac Glandfield Last, happened to be a man of somewhat exceptional gifts for those days. So far as is known young Hardy attended the school for at least six years, going to Dorchester by the high road through the meads, according to a contemporary, who was often his companion.

From all the ascertainable data one must conclude that the education he received at the school of Isaac Glandfield Last was of that rather low standard prevailing in many schools of the type in the country districts in those days. It was said that there were sometimes fewer than half-a-dozen pupils.

But from the character and attainments of his old schoolmaster, as described by those who knew him, there can be little doubt Hardy owed him much. He was encouraged to read useful and good books, which he obtained from a " lending " library at a stationer's shop, kept by a Mr. J. Foster in Cornhill. It was afterwards kept by the Misses Case, who told me that Hardy borrowed many books from the original proprietor. Among them Dumas's historical novels, Scott's novels, and educational books. And in later years he was still a subscriber to the circulating library.

His mother was obviously troubled concerning his education for we learn that when he left school at the age of fourteen, she for several years, strove hard to give him some sort of education of a more adequate type. She purchased for him the classics of Latin writers in the original tongue, and Hardy also had translations to assist him to read them. A little time after he left school, too, a French governess was engaged to give him lessons, and possibly her instruction materially assisted Hardy to become, in after years, the more than competent French scholar that he was, and fostered his future love of French literature.

There is no question that at this particular period of his life he was by various means acquiring a great deal of special knowledge, and of learning of a varied kind. He certainly was destined to prove one of those who learn what is most useful, after they have left the school that was supposed to have educated them.

A close study of him at this period of his life I think cannot fail to prove that his keen and retentive mind during the time intervening between his leaving school and departing for London to follow the profession of architect, must have been employed in acquiring a considerable amount of knowledge of the Wessex peasantry, farmers and townsfolk, and of country life in general, which proved for him of the greatest value as a writer.

Though when at school he was described, in after years by one who knew him, as being " by no means a brilliant pupil ; rather indolent, also not easily led. And, indeed of a meditative disposition, as though in search of something outside his work at school."

He early, however, showed signs of a leaning towards the calling in which he was destined to become so distinguished a member. From what he himself, in after years told the present writer, it was manifest that, in more senses than one, he largely educated himself, and from his mother he received valuable help.

From an old friend of Hardy's, who was a frequent visitor to his home, when he was a young man and Hardy was a child, one gathers our informant thought that much of the material used in both his novels and poems had been acquired by his very careful listening to the conversation of the many friends the family had, and to that of even the serving maids and villagers

His grandmother was a great narrator of reminiscences of her early life ; of gossip ; and of folk tales and striking incidents that had happened in the village, in Dorchester, and the country round about. Several of which happenings were woven into the fabric of the *Wessex Tales*, *Life's Little Ironies*, and form the basis of several of the *Wessex Poems*.

An interesting and valuable sidelight on his character, and of the possession of his latent talent for writing, is afforded by Hardy's own account of how when quite a young boy, owing to his ability to write well, he was employed by the village girls, and even by some in Dorchester, to write their letters and love letters for them. In those days it was not often that the village boys and lasses were able to write legibly, or express themselves adequately.

Doubtless Tess of the D'Urberville's wonderful and appealing letter to Angel Clare, after he had deserted her, had its genesis in the days when Hardy had acted as amanuensis to the girls chiefly, and some boys of Upper Bockhampton.

Evidence of the truth of the story may be taken to be afforded by Hardy himself in *The Mayor of Casterbridge* where Mother Cuxsom, addressing Richard Newson, remarks : " Love letters ? Then let's hear 'em good soul . . . Lord, do ye mind, Richard, what fools we used to be when we were younger ? Getting a schoolboy to write 'em for us ; and giving him a penny, do you mind, not to tell other folk what he'd put inside, do ye mind ? "

It was undoubtedly during the years between the time of his leaving school, and of that when it was decided that he should become an architect that young Hardy was busily employed studying Nature, and those characters with whom he was brought in contact. Remaining a retiring, self-centred and shy lad, who seemed to have been chiefly interested in the natural forces which he observed dominating the fields of Wessex, and in the great stretch of grim, but beautiful, heath, commencing just above his home, where he walked and lay in the heather reading a book, watching the lizards and other creeping things, and listening to the songs of the larks carolling in the sky above him.

Also, perhaps, turning over in his alert and receptive mind the human characteristics which made up the life, and the vital and conflicting emotions, which were his environment.

When he had reached the age of about sixteen his father and mother appear to have become suddenly concerned regarding the apparent futility and aimlessness of the life that Hardy was leading.

They were not in a position to send him to a University ; even if their ambition or wish had prompted them to do so. Nor did I ever discover that Hardy, himself had any desire to go ; nor did he express, in after years, any regret that he had been deprived of the kind of scholarship a University was capable of imparting.

So far as is ascertainable his father would have been quite content for Hardy to have entered his own business, or for him to have taken up farming, or followed some commercial or industrial occupation. His mother, however, following up her ambition, which had led her to give some thought regarding his education after he had left school, put her veto on any of the forms of employment mentioned.

She evidently had in mind for him a position superior to that attained by her husband, and in the end a way out was discovered, and after several consultations with a Mr. John

Hicks, a Dorchester architect, who on various occasions had had business relations with Hardy's father, it was arranged that the boy should be apprenticed, or, as one nowadays expresses it, articled to Mr. Hicks.

Doubtless the Hardy's felt that at all events adopting this course would mean their son taking a step up on the social ladder. And as it happened, just then, there had been a distinct revival of interest in the condition of a number of Dorsetshire churches, and those of neighbouring counties, which had been permitted to fall into a state of disrepair or worse. And as a consequence funds were being raised, so that repairs, and, in some cases, partial rebuilding, might be undertaken.

These facts must have led both Mr. Hicks, and the Hardy's to regard the step taken by the latter as indicating the probability of a busy time for the profession that young Hardy was entering. As a matter of fact several commissions had come into the office of Mr. Hicks of a substantial nature, and others were pending.

Hardy fell in readily enough with the plans of his parents; and, indeed, he had gifts, so it proved, of an artistic nature; which indicate that had he pursued architecture instead of adopting literature as his life's work, he might have done well at the former.

Not much is known of Hardy's first employer, but there seems little doubt that he indirectly exercised a considerable influence upon the life and destiny of his pupil. But it is a rather remarkable circumstance that this, hitherto obscure, country architect, with whom Hardy became associated, should be carrying on his work when there came about an extraordinary amount of interest taken in the state of the ecclesiastical buildings throughout the West of England.

During the earlier part of the nineteenth century, especially during the Napoleonic Wars, people's minds had been too much occupied—and the tension been too great—to permit of much attention being devoted to the condition of the country churches.

To a certain extent Hardy must have heard first-hand accounts of this state of the countryside during his boyhood, and it must be remembered that Dorchester was only a few miles from the sea coast, at a time when there was so much excitement and unrest inseparable from acute fears of invasion. These first-hand accounts which he remembered, he doubtless incorporated into the vivid pages of his *The Trumpet Major*. There were, indeed many people in Dorchester and the surrounding villages at the time when Hardy was storing his memory with the " atmosphere " of Wessex in the throes of great and feared events, who had been eye witnesses of the visit of George III and his court to Weymouth (Budmouth) and also of the historic Review of the troops which had been held on the downs.

Hardy had a busy time while with Mr. Hicks, and the reckless manner in which much restoration and rebuilding work had been carried out Hardy lamented to me on several occasions. But the training he received in overseeing and studying this work served him well in after life.

At one time there existed many drawings and sketches he had made during this period, which exhibited the presence of distinctive merit. His regret for the recklessness and destruction that so often had prevailed never left him. And his sensitive nature and interest in all historic and artistic survivals caused him to express it on several occasions, especially at the General Meeting of the Society for the Protection of Ancient Buildings, held June 20th, 1906.

His sympathy with the poor—always keen—was manifested in the address that he gave on that occasion, when he said, regarding the destruction of memorials and the uprooting and casting aside of tombstones, " It was more often the stones of the poor inhabitants, purchased and erected in many cases out of scanty means—that suffered most." And in the poem

" The Levelled Churchyard," found in *Poems of the Past and Present*, he voiced this point of view.

While with Mr. Hicks his classical studies, which his mother had always encouraged, were fortunately for him pursued. For one of his fellow pupils by the name of Barlow, of whom he had made a friend, had similar tastes to his own, and for two or three years they appear to have studied together. In addition to reading some of the classics, among these Homer and Virgil, they also read the Greek Testament together. And, the first Mrs. Hardy once told me that her husband had kept up his reading of the latter almost daily.

For the period just referred to no biographer can definitely state much regarding his development, or anything of special interest regarding his mode of life. He was now a man ; and is known to have made several other friendships with young students.

On the termination of his apprenticeship to Mr. John Hicks, Hardy decided to try his fortune in London. Soon after reaching London he became acquainted with a Mr. John Norton, who gave him an introduction to Mr. Arthur Blomfield, a Church architect of note, who was afterwards Knighted. While with him Hardy came under the influence of Sir Gilbert Scott, and he attended classes of lectures given by him.

Little is known of Hardy's social life in London ; or of his associates. It is almost a shut book. But there is little doubt that some of the incidents or, at least the mental impressions which he received during those five years he passed in London, can be traced in the pages of his earlier novels. Especially, in his first—never published novel, entitled *The Poor Man and the Lady*.

But the deep impressions made upon Hardy's mind while working with John Hicks at Dorchester, his work with Arthur Blomfield, and later with a Mr. G. R. Crickmay, of Weymouth, in Church restorations, can be traced in the pages of several of his novels. And, for sometime prior to his going to

Weymouth, he had been experimenting with verse, also commencing the groundwork of a novel to which he ultimately gave the title of *The Poor Man and the Lady*—a Story with no Plot, containing some original verse, By the Poor Man.

He had also written a number of poems while he was with Blomfield in London. But few of these appeared in print as paid contributions, until he had gained some reputation as a novelist. Fortunately, in after years, he was able to find copies of some of these earlier poems, and was able to write others from memory. These were ultimately gathered together and published in his volume of verse *Wessex Poems* in 1898.

His first novel already mentioned was finished on July 25th 1868, and was at once sent to Macmillans. Hardy had adopted the pseudonym of " A Poor Man." Within a fortnight the manuscript was returned to him accompanied by a long letter from Mr. Alexander Macmillan, who stated he had read the story carefully, and " with much interest and admiration, but feeling, at the same time, that it has what seem to me drawbacks fatal to its success, and what I think, judging the writer from the book itself, you would feel even more strongly to its truthfulness and justice." The letter continued " much of the book seems admirable, and even full of power and insight." Adding, by way of further criticism, " The utter heartlessness of *all* conversations you give in drawing-rooms and ballrooms about the working-classes, has some ground, I fear, and might justly be scourged as you aim at doing ; but your chastisement would fall harmless from its very excess."

In the autumn of the same year Hardy did something towards re-writing portions of the book, and in December went to London to see Mr. Macmillan. They had a talk concerning the novel ; but the publisher did not even then see his way to issue the book.

However, Mr. Macmillan advised Hardy to see what he could do with the firm of Chapman and Hall.

His interview, when he called to see the principal of that firm in December, did not appear to be to him very promising, but he left his manuscript. And in January, having heard nothing he went to London again. He saw Mr. Frederick Chapman, and in the end the latter told him the firm could not see their way to publish the novel unless Hardy would be prepared to pay the sum of twenty pounds towards the cost. This he agreed to do ; and returned to Dorchester to await the proofs.

These did not materialise, and after a little time he heard from the publishers that they would like to see him. He went up to town, and found that the reader, to whom the manuscript had been given, was no less a personage than George Meredith.

He told Hardy that the firm was prepared to carry out the agreement, but that he himself thought that it would be unwise of Hardy to publish the story, as even now, after revision, it had too strong an element of Socialism, which would render it liable to be attacked vigorously by the reviewers, and that possibly his future would be seriously jeopardized. Meredith appears, however, to have told Hardy that he had gifts, and that the book was, in several ways promising.

It was in fact a satire on country society, the nobility, London Society and the failings and foibles of the middle classes. Also on Christianity as it was then regarded and practised ; in addition ran a tilt against political and domestic morals. Moreover the novel was described by Meredith as " revolutionary."

In the end Hardy took away his manuscript, possibly with the idea of giving consideration to the advice that Meredith had given, and the points that he had raised.

One piece of advice Meredith had proferred was that he should lay it aside altogether, and try his hand at a much less controversial and, in his opinion "dangerous" book, with a more well-worked out plot than that of *The Poor Man and the Lady*.

It is quite possible that Hardy was himself surprised that he should have written what had been characterised as a "dangerous" novel, and, indeed, while writing it had also been concerned with poetic expression, and was quite unconscious of any definitely "revolutionary" predilections.

At all events the novel was put aside, forgotten; and actually disappeared except for a few pages, possibly, of the original draft, which in long after years were found in an old box. Hardy himself could never recall what had really happened to it. Probably he had troubled no further about the manuscript, and had put it away and forgotten it, as he quite frequently did with his poems and other work.

Meredith had given Hardy some encouragement; as well as advising him to cast aside the novel which he told Hardy could not fail, if published, to injure his future prospects.*

It was while in London, on several occasions when he had to interview the firms of Macmillan and Chapman and Hall, that he heard of the death of his first employer Mr. John Hicks.

He returned home, and soon afterwards received a letter from a Mr. G. R. Crickmay of Weymouth, who had purchased

---

*While the concluding pages of this present book were being written, a letter was published in the *Sunday Times*, dated June 8th, 1947, from Sir Newman Flower. In it he refers to a statement, in a previous issue, that Hardy's novel *The Poor Man and a Lady* had never been published. He further writes "I have a copy of it. I showed my copy to Hardy on one occasion, and he told me that the novel was stolen, and published in America, and that he never had a penny or a dime for it."

Sir Newman Flower subsequently wrote to the *Sunday Times* as follows "I find that the book in question was *not* "The Poor Man and the Lady" but the American printed edition of "The Romantic Adventures of a Milkmaid," published in New York in 1883. It appears that Sir William Cockerell, Thomas Hardy's executor had the manuscript of "The Poor Man and the Lady" bound in full morocco for Thomas Hardy, but later the latter burnt it."

the business of Mr. Hicks.   The letter asked Hardy to come to Weymouth to see him.

In the end it was arranged that Hardy should help in the carrying out of several contracts for Church restorations and rebuilding, entered into by Mr. Hicks, which had already been started.   Hardy was to work at the Dorchester Office for three months.   This period was extended, and then Hardy agreed to go to Weymouth to work in Mr. Crickmay's own office.

During his stay in Weymouth he devoted much of his spare time to literary work, which it was by that time quite clear was his natural bent.   Practically nothing is known of his social life while at Weymouth, but he put on record that he did some boating, and from frequent bathing became an expert swimmer.   Also that, in company with a young man, with whom he had become acquainted, he attended a " quadrille " or, as we nowadays call it, a dancing class.

He was at this period busily engaged on a new novel. Indeed, when he had finished the work for Mr. G. R. Crickmay he lived on in lodgings at Weymouth, and continued to work hard at writing the novel, to which he had given the title of *Desperate Remedies*.   The scene of which is principally set at Knapwater House, identified as Kingston House, near Stinsford ; at Weymouth, with some of the minor scenes laid at Dorchester, Southampton and in London.

During the periods of his living at Weymouth, a seaside resort of some popularity even in those days, there is little doubt that Hardy was keenly interested in and observant of the life going on around him.   Storing his mind with scenes in the immediate neighbourhood, and characteristics of the people with whom he came in contact.   Of the people he knew, and those who knew him well while residing at Weymouth practically nothing has been discovered.   Although, many years ago the present writer came across a fisherman whose father

Weymouth

"Budmouth Regis"

Douglas Snowdon

remembered Hardy at the time he lived by the sea, and who hired him boats.

One can, however, find memories of his stay there in his poem called *At a Seaside Town in* 1869, which appears in the collection of his poems entitled *Moments of Vision*, in which we have pictures of the chalk cliffs of Osmington Mills and onwards to Lulworth, or as Hardy calls it " Lulstead " Cove . . . also of the breezy greetings of, and the haltings for talks with the Weymouth fishermen, described by him as " keen sea salts," and even a mention of the town band. Another of his poems, *The Dawn After the Dance*, is doubtless reminiscent of his Weymouth experiences at the " quadrille " class.

In February 1870 Hardy, while hard at work finishing his novel at home, received a letter from Mr. Crickmay asking him to go down into Cornwall, to make drawings and obtain particulars of a church that he was engaged to restore or rebuild. Hardy wrote and refused the offer of work. But in March, when the architect wrote again pressing him to go, having finished *Desperate Remedies*, except three or four chapters, he consented to undertake the work offered.

He finished the story before leaving home, and sent it off to Mr. Alexander Macmillan the following day. And on the Monday he left for St. Juliot, near Boscastle.

Unimportant as this architectural work may have appeared to Hardy, when compared with his literary ambitions, it was, however, destined to have an important and lasting effect upon his future life.

At the Rectory he met Miss Emma Lavinia Gifford, the daughter of Mr. J. Attersoll Gifford, a solicitor. The rector of St. Juliot's parish was the Rev. Caddell Holder, M.A., Miss Gifford's brother-in-law. She was also the niece of Dr. E. Hamilton Gifford, Canon of Worcester, and later Archdeacon of London.

Regarding Hardy's coming to St. Juliot the first Mrs. Hardy left an interesting description.

Among her "recollections," which were found after her death, she recorded the interest and even excitement that was caused in the remote Cornish village, at that time some sixteen miles away from the nearest railway station, by the coming of the architect who was to supervise the work upon the Church.

Miss Gifford, as it happened, had to receive him alone . . . She records how she was struck by his familiar appearance " as if I had seen him in a dream," and she noted his soft voice, and different accent to that to which she was accustomed. And added " So I met my future husband." Here is the picture she drew of him. " I thought him much older than he was. He had a beard, and a rather shabby greatcoat, and had quite a business appearance. Afterwards he seemed younger, and by daylight especially so."

The diarist had noted when he came that he had a blue paper sticking out of his pocket. But this proved, not a plan but a poem !

During the ensuing time that Hardy was at St. Juliot Miss Gifford paid many visits to the church where he was at work, which, she rather naively wrote were " of deep interest to both, and merged in those of further acquaintance and affection, to end in marriage," but not till four years later.

After Hardy had finished his work of making sketches and taking details of what had to be done to the building, he paid several visits to St. Juliot. And when he finally left, he and Miss Gifford kept up a correspondence.

On his return to Weymouth, to complete the drawings of the Church, and the sketches which he had made at St. Juliot, Hardy was destined to meet with another check to his literary aspirations. In April 1870 Messrs. Macmillan wrote saying that they were sorry ; but they were unable to publish his novel *Desperate Remedies*. The decision was probably owing to the nature of some of the incidents occurring in the book. Including the murder of his wife by Æneas Manston, one of the chief characters ; and his being the illegitimate son of the chief feminine character in the story, the lady owner of Knapwater House.

Hardy then sent the manuscript to the firm of Tinsley, which very promptly made Hardy an offer. It was, however, not entirely completed. A synopsis only of the two last chapters had been sent.

Hardy wrote and asked for the return of the manuscript, and Miss Gifford made a fair copy of the whole novel. The book was then sent to Tinsley at the end of the year, and an agreement was come to that, if Hardy would pay seventy-five pounds towards the cost of production, the publishers would put it in hand. If the book was a success and paid expenses, it was agreed that Hardy should be repaid the seventy-five pounds.

On March 25th, 1871 *Desperate Remedies* appeared in three volumes ; and it was on the whole favourably received. But unfortunately the *Spectator* launched a bitter attack upon it, on the ground of the illegitimacy incident. And by this review the book was probably killed.

When the accounts were made out, it was found that only 370 sets had been sold out of the 500 printed, and Hardy was left indebted to the extent of £15. He had the further discouragement of one day seeing copies of the book in three volumes, on Messrs. W. H. Smith and Son's bookstall at Exeter for half-a-crown.

Even this rebuff did not discourage Hardy, though I always regarded him as a very sensitive man. He was disappointed with the result ; but he had already got to work on another novel, which was destined to establish him at least as a writer of unusual gifts.

When the story was completed he despatched it to Mr. Frederick Macmillan. His original title was *The Mellstock Quire*, with a sub-title *A Painting of the Dutch School*. While Hardy had been in London he had visited a number of the picture galleries and collections of pictures, and had been deeply impressed by the work of Dutch masters.

Hardy was not, I think, very happy in his selection of some of his titles, for several of them were altered at the suggestion of his publishers. And two or three bore different titles to those used when he stories appeared in serial form.

Again Hardy was unfortunate, for he misread Macmillan's letter sent him regarding the book. So he wrote and requested the manuscript should be returned. In fact the firm's letter had stated that they were willing to publish the book. But it was returned to him as requested, and with his usual carelessness Hardy put it aside.

Tinsley, the publisher of *Desperate Remedies*, notwithstanding the comparative failure of that novel, had faith in Hardy's work, and shortly after Hardy had received back the manuscript from Macmillans, Tinsley wrote and asked Hardy whether he had another novel. Hardy replied that he had a new novel finished, but could not at the moment say where he had put it !

Tinsley proved insistent, however, possibly having in Hardy ' scented ' a coming novelist, who would do well for his firm. In consequence of Tinsley's persistence, Hardy wrote to his mother asking her to look for the manuscript and, if found, to send it to him. Sometime in April he received it from her ; and he sent it off to the publisher. In the end Tinsley offered to give thirty pounds for the entire copyright, which Hardy accepted. He was, however, paid a further sum of ten pounds—half the amount which Tinsley had received from the German firm, for the rights to publish the novel in the famous Tauchnitz library.

All this while Hardy was still dallying with architecture, reluctant perhaps to take the plunge, and cut himself adrift, until he was able to support himself by his pen. He did quite a number of competition drawings, while he remained in

London, and occasionally did work for Arthur Blomfield, in Adelphi Terrace.

Tinsley published the novel in May 1872 with the title of *Under the Greenwood Tree*, a much more descriptive and attractive one than *The Mellstock Quire*, the title Hardy had chosen. The book was well received ; and, as a result, the firm who were at that time publishing *Tinsley's Magazine*, to which a number of the best-known novelists and writers, at one time or another, contributed stories and articles, wrote to Hardy, and asked whether he would write a serial story to run throughout the yearly volume.

Hardy was getting more used to dealing with publishers, and, before accepting any offer he acquainted himself with the Law of Copyright. As a result he went to see Tinsley, and said that he was not prepared to sell all rights, for which the publisher had offered him £30. After some discussion Hardy agreed to accept the offer for the serial rights, and those for a three volume edition.

The novel for *Tinsleys Magazine* was written very rapidly, partly in London. And then, when he was not finding he could write sufficiently quickly, as he was carrying on some architectural work at·the same time, he went home to Bockhampton to finish the story, which he had named *A Pair of Blue Eyes*. The action, it will, doubtless, be remembered, takes place on the Cornish coast not far from Tintagel, and doubtless Hardy had absorbed the local colour, and become acquainted with the types of character he depicted, during his work relating to the restoration of the Church of St. Juliot, and the subsequent visits he paid to Cornwall when he stayed at the rectory.

Soon after the publication of *Under the Greenwood Tree*, and no doubt because of the nature and success of the book, Hardy was approached in September 1872 by Leslie Stephen, a well-known figure in literary Society, and the editor of the *Cornhill Magazine*. He wrote Hardy and told him he had read

Under the Greenwood Tree, had liked it, and would be pleased if he would write a story for him of that particular type, as he thought it would probably be suitable for serialisation in the *Cornhill Magazine*.

How slender was the chance of Leslie Stephen making contact with Hardy is revealed by the fact that there was, in those days, no regular delivery of letters at Bockhampton. The Dorchester postmaster relying upon them reaching the Hardys, or, indeed, any other of the villagers, by the hand of neighbours who happened, when in Dorchester, to call in at the Post Office.

As it happened, Leslie Stephen's letter had been given to one of the school children, who dropped it in the lane leading to the village. And, had it not been picked up by a passing labourer, who brought it to the Hardy's cottage, it might never have reached its destination. This letter may rightly be said to have had a great influence upon Hardy's future.

The serial *A Pair of Blue Eyes* in *Tinsley's Magazine* proved a success, as did the novel when published in volume form after the story had finished running in the Magazine.

This may be noted as the first real success with which Hardy had met as a novelist.

He had immediately set about writing a successor, which he named *Far from the Madding Crowd*.

At the end of September Leslie Stephen received as much of the manuscript of the story as Hardy had completed. He soon wrote to him that the novel was " just what had been required," adding that it was not usual finally to accept a story until the whole of it had been submitted, and had been read. But it had been decided to make an offer for it based on what had been received. Hardy was very pleased, at the decision and he accepted the offer for the purchase of the novel.

As to Hardy's method or working. He once told me how, when wandering about the countryside, ideas often came into his head when he had not a scrap of paper upon him. Under such conditions he said that he would pick up large dead leaves, chips of wood left by woodcutters, or even pieces of slate, and jot down upon these unusual writing materials notes of the thoughts that had come into his head.

There are numberless entries in Hardy's diaries which disclose how closely he kept in touch with and studied not only Nature from early boyhood, but also the natural forces and characters with which he was brought in contact. And from their fragmentary nature there is evidence that these notes were probably made on the spot, while the impression was fresh and the incident striking.

It was the general practice at the time of the publication of Hardy's serial in the *Cornhill Magazine* for the story to be illustrated. Hardy had, however, some misgivings as to whether the artist would be sufficiently acquainted with the scenic Wessex background of his novel; or be familiar with the types of characters presented to enable him to make satisfactory illustrations. On this point he wrote to Leslie Stephen telling him that, if necessary, he himself could furnish rough sketches likely to be of service to the artist.

Once more Hardy got into trouble by reason of incidents in the story and his way of dealing with them. He, with all his courtesy and kindliness, was always " in the habit of calling a spade a spade." And while the novel *Far from the Madding Crowd* was running as a serial in the *Cornhill Magazine*, Leslie Stephen, the Editor, felt compelled to write to Hardy regarding an incident concerning Fanny Robin and her love episode with Sergeant Troy. He asked Hardy to deal with such incidents in " a more gingerly fashion." Some readers it was assumed had made complaint regarding the incident.

Hardy always found his inspiration most active and did his best work in the country, as might well be supposed, when one considers his origin, early environments and the deep interest he had from boyhood in Wessex and its countryfolk. And, therefore, as soon as *Far from the Madding Crowd* had started running in the *Cornhill Magazine* he went back to his home at Bockhampton to finish the other instalments.

Hardy had also been warned by Leslie Stephen that too great freedom of expression, in such episodes as those noted, might get him into trouble.

A prophecy that came true of his two subsequent outstanding novels *Tess of the D'Urbervilles* and *Jude the Obscure*. Both in their day aroused considerable hostile criticism in some sections of the Press, and also in Religious and Society circles. Especially was this the case with *Jude the Obscure* which was destined to be his last novel.

Relative to the criticism the book received in Great Britain, and there was some of the same kind in the United States, he once said to me that the critics both great and small had altogether missed the intention of the novel and its lesson.

He was particularly incensed by the story that got about after a prominent churchman, the Rt. Rev. W. W. How, who was suffragan of Bedford, wrote to the papers stating that he had put Hardy's novel on the fire in his study.

Hardy was, himself, rather sceptical regarding the current statement, remembering that it was not usual to have fires in summer, and the undoubted difficulty the writer of the letter, who was afterwards Bishop of Wakefield, would have had in destroying so thick a volume in the way he had claimed to have done.

However, Hardy said with a wry smile " better books than mine have been burned." And he took no personal steps in the matter. But the militant Bishop was able to do Hardy's pocket considerable injury, for he wrote to Messrs. W. H. Smith and Son, pointing out what he conceived as " the evil tendency of the book."

As a result of the Bishop's letter, the firm withdrew the novel from their almost innumerable circulating libraries ; and also stopped the sale at their hundreds of bookstalls. And, it was said at the time that the firm assured the Bishop that " any other books by the same author would be carefully examined before they were allowed to be circulated."

There were, however, people of discrimination who recognised in *Jude the Obscure* great qualities and dramatic power, which, even with the obloquy showered upon the novel from certain quarters, and the general gloom and tragedy of the story, might have been ranked as Hardy's greatest and most popular work of fiction.

There were, however, some reviews of an appreciative character by writers who obviously had sensed the power and real object and meaning of the book. And to one of these reviewers, whose identity was not, so far as the present writer is aware, disclosed, Hardy wrote an appreciative and explanatory letter worth recalling. It ran as follows :—" Your review is the most discriminating that has yet appeared. It required an artist to see that the plot is almost geometrically constructed —I ought not to say constructed, however, for beyond a certain point, the characters necessitated it, and I merely let it come. As for the story itself. It is really sent out to those into whose souls the iron has entered, and has entered deeply at some time of their lives, but one cannot choose one's readers."

Hardy went on to say, with a modesty that was, I had learned, characteristic of him " You have hardly an idea how poor and feeble the book seems to me, as executed, beside the idea of it I had formed in prospect."

In a postscript, Hardy, evidently bearing in mind that some critic had labelled the story " grimy," wrote " The grimy features of the story go to show the contrast between the ideal life a man wished to lead, and the squalid real life he was fated to lead . . . . . This fact was meant to run all through the novel. It is a fact, to be discovered in *everybody's* life, though it lies less on the surface, perhaps, than it does in those of my poor puppets."

Jude the Obscure was, so far as fiction was concerned, the final expression of his philosophy, which had earned for him the reputation of being a pessimist, and exhibited once more an example of his obsession regarding Fate.

What he most resented among the avalanche of reviews and press cuttings, of which he was the recipient, was the statement of some paragraph and 'gossip' writers that the novel was largely auto-biographical.

He made no reply to such statements at the time. But many years afterwards he wrote, in reply to a letter from a correspondent, asking whether there was any foundation for such a statement, "there is less of my own life in *Jude the Obscure* than in any of my books."

To the present writer he stated and wrote "There is more of an autobiographical interest—if you care about such matters—in my poems than in the whole of my novels."

As was the case in several of his other novels, there were incidents in *Jude the Obscure* that had occurred in real life, and had become known to him, or of which he had heard. And, as a manifestation of his remarkable gift of memory, he mentioned that the fabric of the book was suggested to him by a youth that he had once met on his way to school, which must have been at least half-a-century before.

While writing this book a letter reached me from a friend who is an admirer of Hardy. It called my attention to an American book upon the great novelist. In the United States, as I know from the correspondence that has come to me from across the Atlantic from time to time, there is a great and abiding interest in Hardy and everything relating to him.

In the book to which my attention was drawn, one of many written by Americans, there is, in connection with *Jude the Obscure* an interesting statement concerning the first Mrs. Hardy's attitude towards the novel. It may be remembered that she came of a well-known family, members of which were intimately connected with the Church of England; several being clergymen of varying distinction. And I have always felt, notwithstanding her support in its early days of the Votes for Women movement, that she was distinctly of a mid-Victorian temperament. And for this reason I am a little doubtful of the authenticity of the American author's statement regarding her attitude towards her husband's last novel. But I admit that she was, from her Church connections, and outlook on life hardly likely to regard so ' strong ' a book with favour.

The statement regarding her attitude avers that she, distressed by the hostile reception of the novel, and Hardy refusing to take any action such as she wished, made a special trip to London, and appealed to Dr. Richard Garnett, the Dean of Letters of the British Museum, for his assistance to aid her in getting Hardy to burn his manuscript. She had already written to Dr. Garnett without avail. On her visit, the American author, mentions that " she implored him " . . . . " she wept."

The story the author also adds " Got about," and that Mrs. Hardy's visit was a fruitless one.

Personally I do not credit this story ; as there are gaps regarding dates.

Hardy's own decision not to write another novel, in consequence of the reception accorded to *Jude the Obscure*, had been taken with promptness, after the position had been carefully considered by him.

It is known, however, that Hardy had for some time previously expressed his dissatisfaction with fiction as a means by which he could express himself.

My own opinion, however, remains that it was not so much the hostility of the critics, and the widespread antipathy to the book shown by a large section of the reading public that led to his decision, so much as it was that he deemed he had failed in his intention, and had been misunderstood.

It is almost certain that he never did write another novel. Though, after his death there were rumours that he had left a posthumous one ; or, had commenced one. Of, which, however, nothing definite was ever heard.

After the publication of *Jude the Obscure*, and his decision to abandon novel writing Hardy was chiefly engaged in collecting together, and editing his early and later poems which had been put away, and unfortunately many of the former, though known to have been written, were never found. He from time to time also wrote some new ones. He was during this period engaged upon and absorbed in the writing of *The Dynasts* which had been simmering in his mind for a long period.

Having read much of Hardy's poetry written and published during the War of 1914-18, and knowing how great an interest he had taken in the War and its repercussions in Wessex and the historic developments of events, I appreciated how evident it was that he had sensed the drama and changefulness, anxiety and sacrifice with which he had been environed.

I, therefore, wrote to him, and ventured to suggest, that in the War, then recently ended, were the materials to his hand for a novel of the *genre* of *The Trumpet Major*, recording a period of National history, perhaps, even transcending in vital interest and importance that of the Napoleonic Era, which he had so vividly described in his other War novel.

In due course he wrote back, thanking me for the suggestion ; but that, although the idea was tempting, he was not inclined to alter his previous decision that he would not write another work of fiction.

That decision may, more than possibly, have deprived English literature of an outstanding and dramatic presentation of the troubled years from 1914 till after the Treaty of Versailles.

Who knows ?

Jude the Obscure was run as a serial in *Harper's Magazine*, commencing in the December number, 1894, and bearing the title of *The Simpletons*. In the January number the title was changed to *Hearts Insurgent*, owing to Hardy's attention having been drawn to the fact that the first title resembled that of another English novel. On the story being published in volume form in the United States in 1895 (though dated 1896), the title was again altered to that by which the novel is now known.

The Well Beloved was first run as a serial, in October to December 1892, in the *Illustrated London News*, with the title of *The Pursuit of the Well Beloved*. On publication, in the United States, in volume form in 1897, the title had been changed to *The Well-Beloved*; and the two versions of the story differed in several particulars.

Strangely enough even this ' fantasy '—as Hardy described it—was by several reviewers fiercely attacked. And by one at least, with what its author called " mendacious malice," and with " Maladroitness as if the writer were blinded with malignity." Hardy stated that the story had been sketched out when he was a young man, many years before it was published. He further explained the idea of the novel in the following words. " There is, underlying the fantasy followed by the visionary artist, the truth that all men are pursuing a shadow, the Unattainable ; and I venture to hope that this may redeem the tragi-comedy from the charge of frivolity."

The Dynasts had long been occupying Hardy's mind, and in 1896 nearly ten years before Part I was published, he was in Belgium with his first wife, and, when in Brussels, visited the field of Waterloo, and made notes likely to be of assistance to him when he commenced seriously to write his great work. He had even then given the latter, in his mind, the provisional title of *Europe in Throes*; and had already decided that the work should be in Three Parts of Five Acts each. He had even jotted down some of the characters he intended to introduce. These included Pitt, Burke, George III, Napoleon, Wellington and many others.

After his Belgian visit he was busy with the first part of *The Dynasts*, and some four years later in 1904, Part I was published, succeeded by Part II, in 1906 ; Part III, and the complete work in one volume in November, 1910.

Those who knew Hardy and his age had been amazed at his energy, industry and diligence in his search for all possible information likely to help him with the writing of the great Drama, and also by the perseverance with which he tracked down all references and incidents likely either to add to the importance or the accuracy of the book.

The reception accorded it was unfortunately by no means favourable as a whole. Most of the critics were faced with a very unusual work of art ; and were quite incapable of adequate and just criticism of it.

Indeed, to some critics, as well as to many other people, it must have presented difficulties inherent from its philosophical basis. And, as a consequence, there was not a great demand for the book.

Originally it had been Hardy's intention not to publish his work until all three sections were completed. But it would appear that he had sent Part I to the publishers after turning over in his mind the pros and cons of his previous intention.

That he was greatly disappointed by the cool reception accorded the book is undoubted. He had, however, at the back of his mind for some time, long before its publication, a doubt as to whether the great work on which he was engaged, and, indeed, had set his heart, would be understood, or accepted as one of importance. A doubt whether it would not be held to run counter to established philosophies and notions. And he feared that the Drama when published, might prove a stumbling block in the way of his being accepted as a poet.

Fortunately for him, however, there were a few of his literary friends capable of recognising the merits of the first Part, and doubtless their appreciation of it cheered him, and encouraged him to complete the other two. It is certain that his friends' appreciation did a good deal to soften the attack made upon the book in some quarters by the least discerning of his critics.

Later on, too, when the whole was available to be considered, critics were more inclined to appreciate some of the more outstanding merits of the work. And, indeed, not a few now admitted its power, and agreed that the Wessex scenes were the true Hardy, and that the country characters were true to life.

With *The Dynasts* completed, published, and off his mind Hardy was for some considerable period engaged in collecting and revising his verses which had appeared in various publications all over the world, and of collating a considerable number of manuscripts, and poems that had been laid aside from time to time, and many of them even forgotten. In some cases he remembered poems that he had written and had not published. A number of these could not be found ; but, in many cases his extraordinary gift of memory enabled him to rewrite them.

Successively, from 1908 onwards, to his two previous volumes of verses *Wessex Poems and Other Verses ;* and *Poems of the Past and Present ;* were added, *Times Laughingstocks and Other Verses ; Satires of Circumstance ; Lyrics and Reveries with Miscellaneous Pieces ; Moments of Vision and Miscellaneous Verses, Late Lyrics and Earlier, with many other Verses, and Human Shows ; Far Fantasies, Songs and Trifles ; and Winter Words.*

Truly a great and rich garnering of inspiration made at the far end of a long life.

Hardy by his novels and by the volumes of verse, just referred to, established himself as one of the great English novelists of the countryside and its characters. Also as a poet of what may, perhaps, best be described as ' vision,' philosophy and of accomplishment.

But what of the man himself ?

The keen and careful student of Hardy's works may arrive at some conclusion from these.

He was undoubtedly a distinguished creative artist of the age in which he lived ; with a remarkable knowledge of what dominated and actuated the characters he depicted in his prose and poetry, and how it was they were what he found them to be. To understand him and what he wrote one must, I think, be prepared to take both Hardy and his ' scene ' for granted. He undoubtedly was, and in his books is, part of that ' scene ' of the Wessex he loved, and so understandingly presented to his readers.

Much has been written concerning Hardy's novels and poems. Much less about him. The criticism of much of his work has always been both hostile and favourable.

At one time, starting with the publication of *Tess of the D'Urbervilles* there existed for some years rival camps of critics. Those of the hostile camp showed by their criticism, in some cases, that they had never ' sensed ' Hardy as he had the people he lived among and described so wonderfully. The other camp rendered a useful and even valuable service in showing how great a writer Hardy really is, and served also to encourage him in his work.

Only those who knew him well personally, and also the countryside and countryfolk he described, could realise how wonderful an achievement his was that he should be able to give life to those Wessex meads, farms, little villages, heaths, hills, woodlands and winding lanes, and to the people dwelling amid these scenes, and also to the forces of Nature that he had so closely studied. So that his readers could often actually visualise them.

He truly created Wessex. I can remember the time when the name Wessex was almost unknown except to students of history. Some people even seemed never to have heard the name. One was met, in the early days of Hardy's literary life, if one used the term Wessex, with the query " Where is this Wessex ? " or the exclamation " Wessex. Never heard of it ! "

44

Blackmore had begun to make readers acquainted with Exmoor; and, a little later, Eden Phillpotts did the same service to Dartmoor by his series of vividly described Devon characters and scenery. But neither of these accomplished writers became personally, as did Hardy, a part of their environment.

Indeed, one fancies that Hardy from early childhood became part of the Wessex scene. That it was, in a word, born and bred in him. More than once a remark of his led me to think that in childhood, when connected thought became possible to him, he was puzzling over what he saw going on around him, and noting the scenes of sheepshearing, harvest homes and laborious agricultural life, which formed his daily background. And wondering what it all meant. Also the other incidents of village festivals, the births, deaths and marriages, the more or less legendary tales he heard his grandmother tell, and the comedies and tragedies of human life with which we know he was brought into close contact.

How soon did he begin to note Life's Little Ironies, and Times Laughingstocks, and The Satires of Circumstance?, which from a study of both novels and poems, one realises undoubtedly served deeply to influence his life and character.

Often he let fall a remark that showed how deep an impression these things made upon his memory even when a child

That amazing memory and tendency to store up impressions of things around him, seems, doubtless, the clue to much that has puzzled those who knew him, and bewildered those who, from time to time, have sought to arrive at a definite conclusion regarding him and his temperament.

Hardy married a second time in 1914; a Miss Florence Emily Dugdale.

Unhappily for those who possibly may have hoped to gain some personal light upon her distinguished husband's character and temperament, her Biography of him is severely impersonal. There is the bare record " In February of the year following (1914) the subject of this memoir married the present writer." That is all.

But, as a record of some interest, it may here be mentioned that Miss Florence Emily Dugdale, was at the time of her marriage, and had been previously for a considerable period, Hardy's secretary. Her father was a Mr. Edward Dugdale, a native of Dorset, then living at ' Riverfront,' Enfield, Middlesex.

Hardy who, at that time was 73, left " Max Gate," on Monday, February 9th, 1914, for London, and the wedding took place on the following day, very quietly, at St. Andrew's Church, Enfield. The only people present, in addition to the bride and bridegroom, were Mr. Edward Dugdale, and Hardy's brother, Mr. Henry Hardy, of " Talbothays," Staffordshire. The Hardy's returned to " Max Gate " the same day as the wedding.

Mrs. Hardy was herself a writer and the author of several books for children.

Her biography is singularly colourless and detached as regards her relationship with him, and it is, indeed, now unlikely that the problem of a great personality will ever be satisfactorily solved. It is, perhaps, not very strange that so little of the true life of Hardy is known. He was a singularly shy man, with a great horror of the publicity that so many, far less distinguished, so urgently seek. And so it was only by casual remarks when in his company, and almost unexpected flashes of self-revelation, that stray threads of knowledge could be woven into an imperfect, though so far as they served, an authentic pattern.

If I may use a modern word, he was by nature an ' isolationalist.' He, as was well-known, hated publicity ; and there was an incident that caused him ever afterwards, if possible, to avoid interviewers.

A young man was many years ago sent down by a London newspaper of some repute to interview him. But he failed to apprehend Hardy; asking him leading personal questions " in an inquisitive and pressing manner." And so got nothing out of Hardy.

The young man went back to London, and wrote an almost entirely imaginative account of the ' interview,' " save for a rather offensive description of his attire and appearance."

Hardy there and then made up his mind not, if it could be avoided, to be interviewed in future. This dislike of publicity was also shown by Hardy's disinclination to be photographed. Few men of distinction such as he attained, I feel sure were less photographed than he.

But he permitted me to take one of him in the garden at " Max Gate " soon after we became acquainted and he was standing near a huge stone that had been unearthed. Hardy thought it might have had a Druidical origin. And I during the time I knew him took other photographs of him in his study, and in the drawing-room at " Max Gate." One of which he chose to be enlarged for a gift to the old Whitefriars Club in London.

I fortunately realised, the first time I met him at " Max Gate," that he would resent being ' drawn.' But if interested in any subject would talk freely about it.

I have written during the passing of many years a good deal concerning him and Wessex. In books, magazines and newspaper articles, both in this country and in the United States.

For several years, after I first got to know him, it was my practice, if I made personal reference to him or of what he had told me in conversation, on cycling and walking expeditions, always to send him an advance copy of my typescript. After a time, however, he said " You need not trouble to send any more typescript, I can rely upon you."

He several times helped me materially with information, and also by identifying, so far as was possible, the places mentioned in his novels and poems.

When I was writing a book upon Wessex in 1905-6 he very kindly promised to glance through the proofs. I therefore sent them to him, and after a short interval they were returned with a kindly comment upon my work, and a suggestion relative to a story that was current regarding an incident which took place in his boyhood. It was that he had once climbed a tree outside Dorchester gaol to witness the execution of a woman for the murder of her husband ; and that a boy friend with him fell down fainting out of the tree, and that Hardy then realised the horror of the scene that he had witnessed.

Hardy wrote at the foot of the proof sheet " The above story, though traditional, may possibly be fictitious." He knew the story had been currently told.

It is of peculiar interest as, may be, it lingered in his memory and inspired, in after years, the dramatic scene, in *Tess of the D'Urbervilles*, outside Winchester gaol on West Hill, when Angel Clare and 'Liza Lu, hand in hand, stood and watched," with their eyes rivetted on the flagstaff," as Hardy put it, to see " a few minutes after the hour had struck, something moved slowly up the staff and extended itself on the breeze. It was a black flag."

" Justice (in Æschylean phrase) was done, and the President of the Immortals had ended his sport with Tess."

When talking with Hardy, one, perhaps slowly, sensed the fact that in reality, there must be two individuals. A delightful companion, more cheerful than reputed ; communicative at times, even sociable, loving Wessex and its history, folklore, people, and the charm that somehow Wessex possesses which to the stranger is so remarkable and alluring. In these characteristics of the man one finds the personality that Dorchester knew, and regarded with some pride and even

respectful affection.   I speak of the ' common people,' and his
fellow citizens that he knew so well.

The other Hardy is less easy of discovery ; or, at all events,
to understand.

As he reached middle life one had only to glance at his
fine profile, with its acquiline nose, and keen eyes ; sometimes, however with a strange sadness temporarily veiling them,
to realise that he had great will power ; would face seeming
defeat (as he several times did when his novels in manuscript
came back refused) and would forthwith set about retrieving
the position and the task of ' winning through.'

Then one, realised if only dimly, the existence of a pro-
found melancholy at times, and a nature that was somehow or
other always at war with itself, with its environment or its
spiritual entity.

His half, and almost shyly hidden force, and powers of
memory and concentration, not only explain his ultimate
achievements, but also lead one to believe that he would have
made his mark in any career that he had deliberately adopted,
and to which he had been irresistably drawn.

In support of this conviction one only has to remember
that as quite a young man, in his first exacting calling of
architecture, he had under the direction of his first employer,
John Hicks, learned much, and afterwards while he was working
in the office of Sir Arthur Blomfield, became the latter's valued
assistant and engaged on several important works including
that of All Saints', Windsor, and Radcliffe Chapel, Oxford.
And that he also became a prizeman of the Royal Institution
of British Architects, winning an award and a medal for an
essay of " The Application of Coloured Bricks and Terra
Cotta to Modern Architecture."

While studying architecture in London he managed to
obtain a University Education at King's College ; thus exhibiting that pertinacity and desire for knowledge that stayed
with him till the last days of his long life.

He went back to Wessex in the end and severed his practical association with architecture, and again took up the study of the scenes in which he had passed his boyhood, haunting Egdon Heath, visiting villages, and beauty spots, afoot, chatting with the countryfolk and with the hucksters of Dorchester Market Place, the shepherds, the labourers, dairy maids and ' tranters,' that he was to bring so vividly alive in his writings.

And one is tempted to imagine how far the extinction of his novel of *The Poor Man and the Lady*, and the initial failures of *Desperate Remedies* and the limited success of *A Pair of Blue Eyes*, may have led to or nurtured the vein of pessimism so easily discoverable in much of his later prose and in a number of his poems.

To have created this overpowering characteristic there must have been in his life some hidden and destructive development of disillusionment to account for it, which served to colour Hardy's vision of Wessex and its characters as he conceived them.

Here are a few suggestions, let them be taken in order as they come to remembrance and mind. Did he discard architecture as a profession because it had served to disillusion him ? One remembers his novel *A Laodicean* had a strong element of architectural interest. One of the chief characters being George Somerset, a young architect, who, like Hardy himself, was at first deeply interested in Gothic architecture, and yet became disillusioned with it, Hardy in the novel puts the following words into Somerset's mouth " all styles were extinct, and with them architecture as a living art."

This novel, it may be recalled has a happy ending ; if one rules out the destruction by fire of Paula Power's home, Stancy Castle, caused by the villain of the story William Dare on the night that Paula, now Mrs. George Somerset, returned to Markton (Dunster) with her husband, to whom she had been reconciled and had married.

For this happy ending, it was said, Hardy repented, describing it as a " predetermined cheerful ending."

He, when on several occasions questioned as to in what manner his characters were arrived at, *i.e.*, what had made him cause them to act in the way they did, replied " They came into being, and more often than not, took command of their development," or " I let them do just so."

In connection with his novels he once remarked " Some of these of Wessex life address themselves more especially to readers into whose souls the iron has entered, whose years have less pleasure in them now than heretofore. And to whom marriage is not the Eternal City but only a milestone on the way."

One day, long years ago, when cycling with Hardy, if my memory serves, something he said on that August afternoon made me think that he was dissatisfied with his home life. And the foregoing statement regarding his novels seems, in a way to confirm the impression made upon me. For one thing he was very fond of children ; and there were none in his home.

Often when with him cycling or walking, his love of them manifested itself when we met any coming out of school. Or when he stopped to chat with some villager, and her own children or others came up. He seemed to be sensed by them as a friend, and when he spoke or patted their heads they smiled back at him.

And, perhaps with memories of his own schooldays and their childish troubles, he would enquire how they liked school, or were doing well at school. They would answer as though they knew him well.

Then as regards his reference to marriage not being the Eternal City.

The first Mrs. Hardy always struck me as just ' unsuited ' to be a distinguished man's wife. She was a lady of a good family with a close connection with the Church and had relatives, several of them distinguished, in its service. She seemed to me that she would have made an admirable Vicar's or Squire's wife of the mid-Victorian age. Looking after the parishioners or tenants ; going about with a basket on her arm, or on the seat of her carriage, containing delicacies for the old or sick people.

She was kindly, friendly and hospitable ; I felt sure that she at times fretted Hardy ; and, at others, often sought to explain him as what he was not. That is to say orthodox ! For orthodoxy was one of her Gods.

Let me illustrate this.

Years ago, in 1903, Madame Sarah Grand, the writer of *The Heavenly Twins*, a novel which had made a great sensation ten years previously, was staying with my wife and me at our Bournemouth home. As Chairman of a Literary and Debating Society in the town, I had invited her to come down and Lecture at the then well-known Winter Gardens Pavilion. The title of her Lecture was the very intriguing one " Things we Forget to Remember—" It was brilliantly delivered.

She was aware that I knew Hardy, and wrote to me a few days before she came to Bournemouth to ask whether I thought I could arrange to take her over to Dorchester to see him. I wrote to Hardy, and an answer came back. " Certainly come, I should like to meet her. Come over to lunch."

And so we went.

Hardy was delightfully cordial in his rather shy way. And Mrs. Hardy, who had read *The Heavenly Twins*, approved it in principle, if not in detail. A few years later, she was destined to take a rather prominent part in the " Women's Suffrage Movement."

At lunch the conversation between Hardy and his distinguished guest ranged widely over the fields of Literature, Art, Music, and in the latter part, theoretical Religion, and was brilliant to listen to. Rapier thrusts from both at shibboleths ; political arguments ; a discussion regarding the responsibility or otherwise of novelists, and the then tendencies of the modern novel. Wessex, and perhaps the weather, which was brilliantly fine.

And after lunch the conversation was continued, less energetically, in the pleasant garden, where we later had tea on the lawn.

I had noticed during the discussion at lunch that Mrs. Hardy was at times inclined to be restive at some of the heterodox opinions expressed by her husband, which I fancied were sometimes made for the purpose of promoting dispute. For both he and his guest did dispute. The former sometimes laughing the while.

During lunch Mrs. Hardy had several times intervened with a gentle denial that what her husband had been saying was his real opinion ; and Sarah Grand noticed this and smiled.

Once or twice, I remember, Mrs. Hardy definitely said " my husband doesn't think that at all."

Then Hardy laughed.

It was a most fascinating experience. A woman's wit and gift of repartee, which Sarah Grand possessed to a marked extent, matched against, perhaps a more logical and introspective type of intellect.

On our way back to Bournemouth Sarah Grand, in discussing the luncheon talk, said how glad she was that she had been able to meet and talk with Hardy. Also that somehow he was not at all the man she had imagined him to be. " Less of a recluse, indeed ; very logical, and I shall always remember him as very human."

Later she remarked how kindly and hospitable Mrs. Hardy appeared to be. Adding, after a slight pause, " But perhaps a little too conventional for a man of the type of Hardy."

Strangely enough I received a letter from Mrs. Hardy during the following day. She was perturbed, doubtless, lest I might at any time quote in conversation, or otherwise, any of the rather unconventional opinions to which Hardy had given expression.

I told Sarah Grand, in part, the contents of the letter, and she smiled, and there was a world of understanding in that smile.

I always remember Sarah Grand's expression that Hardy was " very human." He was ; and was also very humane, which are two quite different qualities.

Until he became famous he was little thought of by the ' gentry ' (I use the word as being the most expressive) of Dorset, which was and still is a hunting and sporting county. Indulging in what Hardy once described to me as ' blood sports ' ; that is to say hunting, shooting, coursing and fishing. I always thought he was a little disconcerted by being for a time ' cold shouldered.' When he won through, and became recognised as an outstanding writer, and a distinguished man, he found himself with the entrée to most houses, and the sought for friend of many distinguished and famous people.

His antipathy to sport of all kinds which involved the killing or suffering of animals he himself expressed in his striking poem *Afterwards*, in which he so strangely foretold, as one might say, ' to the letter ' his own passing away when he wrote :—

> " If I pass during some nocturnal blackness, mothy and warm,
> When the hedgehog travels furtively over the lawn,
> One may say " He strove that such innocent creatures should come to no harm."
> But he could do little for them : and now he is gone."

I always felt that one was nearer to understanding Hardy when alone with him amid the country scenes in which he took so keen and comprehending an interest and pleasure. Of his love and tenderness towards all living, 'innocent' and inarticulate 'creatures' I more than once, when with him, had a manifestation.

I remember one occasion.

We were on our way cycling to High Stoy, and the stone by the wayside which he had promised to show me, that had suggested to him his poem *The Lost Pyx*.

We were riding along in the sunshine of a beautiful August afternoon, and approaching the foot of the hill that led up to the mysterious and legendary column, when a blackbird fluttered out of the hedge, with a broken wing.

Hardy got off his cycle, and, turning after a moment to me a distressed and, indeed, almost agitated face, said " Will you do something for that poor bird ?   I cannot."

I replied " Certainly, if I can.   What is it ? "

He replied, almost turning his head away from the wounded bird, " Kill it."

Adding " If you don't—I couldn't—it will be tortured by a cat or a stoat."

I went to the roadside, and, when I came back to him, he said " Thank you.   Poor thing, poor thing !"

We mounted our cycles.   But soon the hill became steep and he jumped off, saying " You are young, so ride on if you wish.   I am going to walk."

He was nearing seventy at that time.

Before we both started to walk, Hardy, resting his back against the saddle, pointed out to me the beauty of the distant view.

Quite suddenly he looked at me and said " I am going to ask you a question.   Will you answer it honestly ? "

" If it can be answered at all, it shall certainly be answered honestly," I replied.

" Well then," he said, " If you had had the choice of being born, would you have been ? "

In reply I told him that had he asked me the question less abruptly I should probably have answered " Yes." But that he had raised great doubt in my mind. Then I asked him " Would you ? "

After a pause the reply came : " No, surely not." Followed by several reasons, which were weighty enough as the speaker stated them.

The significance of the reply, it should be noted, was that this conversation occurred at the time when he was at the height of his fame as a novelist, as near as I can fix it, some years after the publication of *Jude the Obscure*.

Here had been the admission of pessimism, that undoubtedly existed in Hardy's outlook upon life, of which he himself accepted the description.

Indeed, to one who knew him well there could be little doubt regarding the matter, if one accepted the word as bearing the interpretation usually attached to it. It in a measure explained the pessimism or fatalism which permeates his novels, and many of his short stories in one form or another. They are, however, lightened, here and there, by sly humour, as though he was silently amused by the sorrows, struggles and frailities of humans.

On one occasion he was asked by a correspondent wishing to pin him down on the matter, whether he considered that a pessimist held that the power of evil in the world was greater than that of good.

Hardy replied that he did not entirely accept that point of view. Adding, however, " I know that many people call me a pessimist ; and if it is pessimism to think with Sophocles that ' not to be born is best,' then I do not object to the designation."

His, indeed, was the intellectual pessimism of a logical and searching mind, and not that of a man who is a pessimist by reason of continued frustration of his life's hopes through no fault of his own, and his being seemingly the sport of chance.

On one occasion he contended his novels and poems were not, as an American critic had claimed, " the gospel of pessimism," but declared were " one continued plea against man's inhumanity to men—to women—and the lower animals."

Of his underlying kindliness I have several memories. One in particular. On one occasion I had cycled with him between twenty and thirty miles ; visiting among other places Milborne St. Andrew's (Millpond St. Jude's) which appears both in *Tess of the D'Urbervilles* and *Far from the Madding Crowd.*

As we approached the village Hardy said " We will call in at a cottage and get a cup of tea. An old lady who lives there always makes me one, when I am in this neighbourhood."

The cottage proved a charming thatched one, set back fifty feet or so from the road, which space was occupied by a real cottager's flower garden, with a path up the centre leading to the door and porch.

On both sides of the path were rows of Hollyhocks, Sunflowers, and less striking flowers, Canterbury Bells, Sweet Williams, Candytuft and climbing and dwarf Nasturtiums, while in the background were several rows of Sweet Peas in full bloom.

We met with a cordial welcome when the old lady came to the door and discovered who it was. Greeting him with " Come along in, Mr. Hardy, I be glad to see ye along again this way," adding : " Of course, you'll want a cup of tea, and the gentleman too."

Hardy nodded his head, and after introducing me, sat down in a large ' Windsor ' chair not far from the open hearth.

On the opposite side of the room, near a diamond-paned window, in which I noted there were some pieces of old ' bottle ' glass, a young girl was busily making a dress with a sewing machine. Hardy went over and spoke to her, smiling, and she smiled up at him in return and laughed.

He then came back and said he had found that she was to be married in about ten days' time. He added that he had known her grandmother for many years ; and her from childhood.

I suggested that the dress she was making, which was pale blue, was the actual wedding-dress, Hardy re-crossed the room and bent down and spoke to her. She nodded her head, and blushed deeply.

The old lady had by this time made the tea, and had placed it on the table.

When he came back from speaking to the girl he exclaimed " You were quite right about the dress. But how on earth did you know ? You must be a veritable Sherlock Holmes."

A reference to the stories which had made their author Arthur Conan Doyle famous.

I replied, " I merely guessed from the colour. Very often a country girl, who for one reason or another is not married in a white dress, chooses pale blue, the Virgin's colour, in which to be married."

Hardy smiled, and said " I think I have heard of the custom. It may, perhaps, be traditional."

Then he continued " I have promised to attend the wedding. There seems—she is an orphan, and from childhood has lived with her grandmother—a doubt as to whether her uncle can come to the wedding to give her away, so I have offered to do so."

I subsequently heard he had performed that kindly act.

He was then at the height of his fame, and much sought after by ' Society ' people, and was going out a good deal when in London. Doubtless many of the girls he met in Society circles would have been proud to have had him as a guest at their weddings.

Much discussion has from time to time arisen in the Press regarding the actual localities of the places mentioned in

Hardy's novels and poems ; which he often described with such careful detail.

Talking to him, on one of our cycling expeditions, he told me that many of the villages, places and scenes that he described in his novels and poems were actual, in that they existed very much as he described them, and were only thinly disguised by other names. But he admitted that he sometimes transferred some object or building from its actual site to another position, to make the picture that he drew more in keeping with his imagination of it.

This was the case, for instance, with the observatory which plays a prominent part in his novel *Two on a Tower*. The tragic and somewhat fantastic story of Swithin St. Cleave, the young astronomer, and Lady Vivette Constantine, the owner of Welland House, actually Charborough House, near Wimborne, who fell in love with him. The tower on Rings-Hill Speer, standing above Welland Bottom, and the Gothic tower at Charborough were ' combined ' by Hardy to make the meeting place of Lady Vivette Constantine and Swithin St. Cleeve more possible. The situation of the obelisk at Weatherbury Camp corresponds the more closely with Hardy's description of the observatory used by Swithin St. Cleeve, than does The Charborough Gothic tower. Besides which the obelisk, which Hardy wrote " had been built in the Tuscan order of classic architecture, and was really a tower, which being hollow inside, permitted access to the top."

It was in this tower or obelisk that the meetings of Lady Constantine and her lover are described as taking place.

On another occasion when I went with Hardy to Wellbridge Manor House, which figures so tragically in *Tess of the D'Urbervilles*, we also went across to Bindon Abbey, to see the actual stone coffin, of the Abbot of long ago, in which Angel Clare had placed Tess, after carrying her across the meads.

The dairy farm where Tess was working when she met Angel Clare, was not far away. It was just such a farm as

Hardy had pictured as " Talbothays," and as we leant over the white gate, I remembered the scene in the novel. The name he had given the farm had been suggested to his mind owing to it being that of his brother Henry's home.

There near a holly bush, was the white gate, leading into the barton, and " the long thatched sheds stretched round the enclosure, their slopes encrusted with vivid green moss, and their eves supported with wooden posts, rubbed to a glossy smoothness by flanks of infinite cows and calves of bygone years."

It was the veritable " Talbothays " of the novel.

Only Hardy had given it a name that did not rightly belong to it.

It was on the old Elizabethan Bridge that spans the river Frome at Wool, that Hardy told me the legend, or tradition connected with the D'Urberville family of old.

Perhaps, the day, a beautifully fine and hot one in August, may have destroyed some of the eerieness of the story, which ran as follows.

Some three centuries ago a 'wild' member of the D'Urbervilles abducted a young heiress, and carried her off in his coach to the Manor House which played so tragic a part in Tess's history. The story is that on a certain night in every year a spectral coach comes silently along the road from the direction of Wool, and on reaching the spot nearest to the house, vanishes. It is also stated by tradition that the screams of the unwillingly abducted heiress are heard, by those who pass over the bridge at that hour, if they have any D'Urberville blood in their veins. Only those who have can see the coach.

Hardy told me that he had heard the legend from the lips of several people in Wool, who had claimed to have seen the spectral coach.

When I asked him if he believed the story, he was non-committal ; and merely replied that strange things did happen to some people. One old man told him that he had had "to stand back in one of the recesses of the bridge to allow the coach to pass, and that it was like a cold mist striking him."

I think that Hardy's attitude, towards what is commonly known as the supernatural, is aptly summed up in Hamlet's words spoken to Horatio " There are more things in heaven and earth, than are dreamt of in our philosophy."

Hardy always seemed to me deeply interested in the supernatural ; as well as in Nature itself.

Once discussing the subject of Wessex superstitions with reference to witchcraft, which, at about that time, I believe, some writer had recently been stating still lingered on in Wessex, or had almost died out. Hardy remarked that such beliefs undoubtedly did linger on with some of the older people, although they might not admit it.

When he was a boy, he added, such beliefs were anything but uncommon. And he stated that at the time of which he was speaking he knew of women who would make a figure of anyone whom they adjudged was their enemy, or ' overlooking ' them as it was called ; and would then melt it before a fire or stick pins in it, believing that by so doing the person would suffer a mortal or other injury. And the belief in the evil eye, had even at that time, by no means died out. It will be remembered that in some of his short stories he had used some of the superstitions prevailing as the basis of a tale. For example in that of *The Withered Arm*.

On another occasion he stated that he was really anxious to believe in what is known as the supernatural. Indeed his temperament, and his liking to enquire into and try to solve the inexplicable bears this statement out. He added, perhaps with a challenging smile, that when a young man he would have mortgaged ten years of his life to have seen a ghost. " A real and unquestionable ghost."

He certainly believed that he was of the temperament to see such a thing if it existed.

He said on one occasion that his mother believed that she had seen a ghostly manifestation. It related to a member of the family, who had a child and was herself ill; and fancied she was going to die, and told Hardy's mother so. The latter laughed at the other woman's fears, and, as a matter of fact the sick person recovered.

Some time afterwards his mother was very wakeful, and, although she told him what had occurred, she declared that when it happened she was undoubtedly wide awake. She described how she had seen her relative enter the room, holding the child out to her with a gesture of appeal. Soon afterwards she heard that her relative had died at the precise time of her appearance. There was another strange circumstance that occurred in this connection. The woman when sinking kept repeating that she wished Hardy's mother to have charge of the little one."

"Though I cannot explain how all this happened," said Hardy in conclusion, "I do not doubt that my mother saw what she afterwards described."

I can quite believe, as he once said, that he himself very seriously desired to see a supernatural manifestation, if such things existed. And I think to do so might have resolved his troublous doubts regarding the future life.

Many of my older readers may possibly recall that Hardy was more than once publicly attacked or described as an atheist. And there was at one time quite a considerable discussion of what his religious or other beliefs might be.

As I have already recorded in this study of him, as a man from childhood upwards, his mother and father were what is conventionally described as " religious people," attending Stinsford Church (called by Hardy " West Mellstock ") in the choir of which several members of his family and also neighbours played instruments for a period of more than half-a-century, and those who knew Hardy's mother always

The Hardy Memorial, Dorchester.

held her to be a ' God-fearing ' woman, with a good influence over her children.

And Hardy himself in his middle age and later life used to attend St. Peter's Church, at the junction of High East and High West Streets. I think that it was chiefly his inborn love of music that possibly drew him to attend the services.

After I got to know him well, on several occasions, he referred in a non-committal way to the subject of religion, which caused me, from these and other statements, to regard him as an honest—though by no means a militant agnostic. Or rather perhaps, should I describe him as an earnest and diligent searcher after Truth in regard to God.

The statement made in the second Mrs. Hardy's biography of her husband rather confirms me in this opinion. Referring to the numerous descriptions, as regard his religious opinions, imputed to him by critics and others, she wrote in this connection " he once said—perhaps oftener—that although invidious critics had cast slurs upon him . . . . they had never thought of calling him what they might have called him much more plausibly ——— churchy ; not in an intellectual sense, but in so far as instincts and emotions ruled. As a child, to be a parson had been his dream . . . . He himself had frequently read lessons at the church, and had at one time, as a young man, begun reading for Cambridge with a view to taking Orders."

Hardy's own admission, pathetic, honest and tragically hopeless, as it seems, makes, to my own mind, a very clear picture of what he really was in regard to religion, and the future existence of mankind regarding which, he admitted himself, " obscurely conscious."

He wrote in his diary under the date of January 29th, 1890 " I have been looking for God for fifty years, and I think that if he had existed I should have discovered Him."

Like multitudes of other people, he was undoubtedly much troubled by questionings of the existence of good and evil in the world, and how it should be that evil was permitted by a Deity, who could presumably have so easily checked the evil, and in doing so have given to poor humanity a much better and happier world in which to live.

In these present times attention may, perhaps, be drawn to his expression of an opinion once given " that an end to War could only be brought about by ridicule and a realisation of its stupidity and wastefulness."

And in answer to a correspondent who forecast in 1918 that scientific ammunition-making was only in its infancy (which had been proved to be a tersely prophetic foreseeing) Hardy made the following reply, " I do not think a world in which such fiendishness is possible to be worthy of saving. Better let the Western civilisation perish."

From a poem, written in the year before he died, and reprinted in his *Winter Words*, I quote the last verse, which seems to me to sum up the man I knew and tried to understand.

" And if my vision range beyond
   The blinkered sight of souls in bond,
   —By truth made free—
   I'll let all be.
   And show to no man what I see."

CHAPTER II.

INVITATION TO WESSEX

A GENERATION OR SO AGO, although the genius of Thomas Hardy had done much to make the ancient Kingdom of the West Saxons, known as Wessex, less forgotten by readers of his novels and poems, it was still somewhat a vague land, in that part of England that lies towards the setting sun. A countryside, indeed, less invaded by the ordinary tourist and holiday maker than almost any other equally picturesque portion of Southern England.

It was, of course, not to be found marked as Wessex on the usual maps. One has to go back centuries to find it so delineated. It is, however, to be discovered on some of those beautiful illuminated and interesting maps, which often have pictures of little churches dotted about them, and sometime whales sporting in, and galleons sailing on the narrow seas. Also, often, with the armorial bearings of the landed gentry in full colour ; enlivining and beautifying them.

Nowadays there come to the county of Dorset—to which Thomas Hardy gave the name of Wessex—holiday makers and tourists from far afield, many from the United States, where his work as a novelist and poet is held in high esteem.

As I write it is spring in Wessex.

In the lanes the trees are budding ; and, in the sheltered positions are already bursting into leaf. And here and there on the mossy banks the yellow primroses are already flowering, and wild violets are shyly showing.

The branches of the trees overhead, bare so long it seemed, are about to take on the green mantle that in a week to two's time will be spreading, a picture of loveliness across the countryside. And on the boughs the blackbirds and thrushes are already singing and sparrows have begun to raise their twittering notes in welcome of Spring.

Soon there will be a yellow blazonry of primroses, silver anemones and a shimmering amethystine carpet of wild hyacinths in the shady recesses of coppice and wood. And a little later masses of blackthorn blossom will deck the hedge-rows with a bridal garment of white.

The tiny rivulets, now free at last of icy bonds, commence to sing again their songs, as they ripple over the pebbly beds ; and here and there flash back the gleam of sunlight through the overhanging willows bordering the streams.

Shelley wrote of such a scene as I have in mind, thus :

" The brighest hour of unborn Spring,
    Through the Winter wandering,
    Found it seems, the halcyon morn
    To hoar February born ;
    Bending from heaven, in azure mirth,
    It kissed the forehead of the earth,
    And smiled upon the silent sea,
    And bade the frozen streams be free,
    And waked to music all their fountains."

And, as the sun swings westward at the close of day, in the woodlands as one passes along, one sees the fretted, shadow-tracery of twigs and of branches of the over-hanging trees, as yet only half delivered from the bareness of winter, falling upon the mossy and flower-bedecked earth beneath.

The very spirit of new life has commenced to strew flowers upon the lately barren way, and in Wessex, in Spring, the sheer joy of it is in the air and ambient sunshine ; the blue sky, with banked clouds white and commanding as Alpine peaks, and the sense of Nature's fair awakening.

But it is in the orchards that Spring is most beautiful. The rugged, older trees, which a few months before, in their nakedness and sometimes grotesque growth, seemed to be impossible of beauty, are now bedecked, as are the younger trees, with a garment of pink and white blossom. They have been transfigured, and rendered lovely beyond all other spring-time visions.

And beneath the trees, as the soft breeze blows from off the uplands, one sees a carpet—as it were woven in patches of colour—more exquisite than any yet made for the palace of a queen. A carpeting of green, white and pink ; ghostly at dawn ; fairy-like at sundown. Surely it is at such a time and place that the " little people " of legend and story hold their revels.

> " This is the time when bit by bit
> The days begin to lengthen sweet,
> And every minute gained is joy . . . "

Has sung a poetess.

In the vales through which placid streams meander past willow-clad banks and rush-grown pools—at early dawn mists have hung diaphanous—mists such as those out of which Titania's robe might have been woven ; swirling vapours in fantastic shapes. At first grey and sombre, and then, as the sun creeps up over the environing hills, tinted with all the exquisite colours of the rainbow.

And of such is Springtime in Wessex, when, as Sir Francis Bacon wrote " the breath of flowers is far sweeter in the air where it comes and goes like the warbling of music . . . . and Nature, as yet untired with the labours of a year, is fresh from Winter's sleep, and eager to do her best to rejoice the wayfarer and bring hope anew into the hearts of men."

Upon the steel-grey pools and in the shallow backwaters coots dart to and fro like ebon shuttles, eager for the work of nest-building ; leaving a fan-like wake of ripples behind to mark their course.

On the lofty downs and in the pastures shepherds are busy ; and flocks once more appear to roam at will. Whilst amid the gorse of the moorland, and the heather of the outer wild, the birds are building.

A little later and in the hedges are heard the querulous twitterings of fledglings, and the anxious calls of parent birds which have returned to find their nestlings gone. There are not, perhaps, the joyous full-throated carollings of the year when it was young ; save at dawn and when at last the shadows creep across the fields at the close of day.

Then when Summer comes, with its wealth of flowers, the pilgrim in Wessex will find a new interest both in its scenery and active life. Lanes and by-ways which, but a month or two before, held the promise of rich foliage have made that promise good. The over-arching trees afford a canopy of shade for sun-weary eyes, and the banks and fields provide many a resting place for tired bodies a-tramp.

The hedges are now gay with blackberry bloom, clematis, wild roses and the white, bell-shaped convolvulus. Beside the little wayside rivulets are yellow patches of buttercups ; with king-cups and large daisies in the fields. And the shy violets have yielded place to forget-me-nots. In the banks of the roads now bloom the purple cranebill, blue mallows, crimson-tipped daisies, all half-hidden beneath the long grass, and the fronds of hartstongue and " basket " ferns.

In Summer, too, come to hedgerows and fields new fre-quenters and inhabitants. Many hued butterflies, hovering and flitting from flower to flower and hedgerow to hedgerow. Dainty, fragile things only fit for gentle summer breezes and summer sun. And over the rivers and streams, that thread their way through the meads, gauze-winged dragonflies, with steel-blue and grey-green bodies, flash hither and thither in the sunshine.

In the sunlit vales the cattle are lowing, standing knee-deep in meadow grass, or in some shallow, tree-shaded pool at a river bend. And here and there the grass is falling beneath the hum of machine, or still, here and there, to the rhythmic swing of the scythe and to the mower's song.

In Summer, too, the river has cast the silver of its earlier sheen into Nature's melting pot and now, in the summer sunshine, shows long stretches of dazzling gold. In the shallows the current of the stream plays against the rushes, and, to the listening ear comes the faint hum as of a softly driven spinning-wheel. The coot has long before built her nest and hatched her young, and now sails across the quiet reaches of the river with a flotilla of young ones in her wake.

Sometimes, too, in Wessex, if the wanderer is fortunate he may catch a glimpse of the sheeny kingfisher, watching patiently from a willow trunk with alert eye ; or flashing like a ray of amethyst and emerald downwards to the shimmering water.

In the woodlands, that lie amid the hills, there is a pleasant shade for the weary—the deep shade and silence of the eternal. Underneath is a carpet of flowers in some of the coppices. Those that love the coolness and filtered lights of the woods— find tall foxgloves, white, and speckled pink ; purple flowered wood betony ; and yellow toadflax, with the soft-treading emerald-green mosses and colour-enriched lichens underfoot. And hidden in the upper branches of overhanging leafage the shy birds of the woodlands let fall their songs.

In the recesses of the woodlands there is a dim, restfulness that is grateful to sun-tired eyes.

Away yonder on the high chalk downs, whose rounded bosses, so green in springtime, are now as though tanned by the summer sun, the flocks of sheep are wandering. And now and then one catches the tinkle of sheep-bells (music loved of shepherds who have wandering sheep) and the sound floats down into the vales.

"Cross-in-Hand."
Batcombe Hill.

Douglas Snowdon

On the hills of Wessex the soft breeze of summer murmurs in the early morning ; and by noon is often silent. And at even wakes again. And when the night wind blows it is often scented with the strong and somewhat cloying perfume of gorse on the hillsides, and also the scent of other upland flowers ; wild thyme, brier and pinks.

Night on the uplands is beautiful in summer. The shadow of clouds cast by silvery moonlight chase each other across the surface of the grass. And, if one stands quietly still, one catches glimpses of conies gamboling ; scuttling from their burrows in gorse patches, out of shadows into the moonlight.

In the vales, below the uplands and beneath a star-gemmed sky, the scattered hamlets gradually fade from sight ; and one by one the yellow, star-like lights of homes blink at one from the windows of scattered farmsteads for a time, and then go out one by one, leaving the world wrapped in the blue darkness of a summer night.

Along the Wessex coastline, so varied in its character, the dawn breaks in fine weather with a gorgeousness of colouring that cannot be exaggerated. And the waves make muffled music along the sandy beaches ; and with a sharper note— though muted compared with that of winter—against the rocks and crags. And out at sea the white-sailed ships alas ! gradually decreasing in number—" dream on their silent way."

Summer, the season of flowers brings to the gardens and fields a blaze of colour, and to Wessex gardens a riot of blossom which tells of a rich soil and pure air. Over the thatch of cottages climb roses red and white ; and along the narrow paths leading to the doors nod campanulas and roses. And the mingled scent of stocks, sweet peas and lavender perfumes the air ; whilst often edging the paths are wide-faced yellow sun-flowers and stately rods of white, pink and red hollyhocks.

In such gardens, instinct with colour, perfume and beauty, the town-dweller on holiday seems to find the concentrated joy of summer life, with the hum of bees, and twittering of sparrows from the thatched eves. Many such a garden have we seen in Wessex. Quiet bowers, to use Hardy's title, " far from the madding crowd." Even in these strenuous times—indeed, a spot full of sweet dreams and undisturbed peace.

Autumn, too, brings many beautiful scenes in Wessex. Exquisite tints of the woodland regions ; beauty of clouds and shadows, and the enchantment of lingering summer days. Along the winding lanes there exists a new charm. Overhead the green canopy has changed to one of yellow, russet, crimson, and browns of many shades ; and underfoot the leafy carpet, is thicker day by day. Lingering blackberries give a sombre, or a crimson note to the hedgerows, and the scarlet of the wild rose's fruit is seen on every side. Creepers are " turning " and exquisite autumn tints arc veining all leaves. Nature's rich pencilling for mortal's admiration.

Summer flowers seem still to linger in the hedges as though loth to go with the rest of summer's joys ; and pale forget-me-nots seem to be frailer beside brook and river.

In the orchards golden leaves are falling, to rival, in their carpet of the greensward underneath the trees, the beauty of that of spring. And boughs which bent with blossom are bending now 'neath the weight of russet and sun-kissed crimson fruit.

In the wide fields the nodding corn, yellow-brown is falling in the track of the reaping machines ; though even nowadays, here and there, comes in Wessex the music of the scythe and sickle being sharpened, and the rustle of falling swathes of heavy-headed grain.

In the well-watered vales of Wessex the cattle roam at will amid the grass of which there is a rich aftermath. The river flows along once more a silvery grey, and green where the weeds have grown thick. The water no longer turned to gold as it was in summer sunshine.

The reeds are high along the banks, and they bend reluctantly under the pressure of the water, and the velvety-brown spearheads of rushes, nod gravely in the autumn breeze. The silvery green of the willows is now changed to pale gold ; and at sundown, in this season of mists and mellow fruitfulness, diaphanous vapours enshroud the landscape at sundown.

To the uplands the breath of Autumn has come ; the bracken has put on its brown tints ; the golden glory of the gorse is slowly fading ; and the wild thyme no longer gives out its full perfume. The flocks at night seek shelter for the wind is chill. Below, the woods stretch, a blaze of orange, green and brown foliage ; slowly thinning in the autumn wind.

" The year grows still again, the surging wake
of full-sailed summer folds its furrows up ;
As after passing of an argosy
Old silence settles back upon the sea,
And ocean grows as placid as a cup.
Spring the young morn, and Summer the strong noon,
Have dreamed and done and died for Autumn's sake ;
Autumn that finds not, for a loss so dear,
Solace in stack and garner here too soon—
Autumn, the faithful widow of the year."

In the coppice the nuts are falling earthward from their husks, and the industrious and provident squirrels are already laying in their winter stores.

Here and there in cottage gardens roses linger amid the autumn flowers, and sunflowers traditionally turn their heads towards the waning sun ; reminders that Summer has passed silently away. And from the chimneys of cottages, nestling beneath the hills, blue smoke of wood-fires curls upward— another sign that autumn with its chilly nights is here.

William Barnes, known to Hardy when a boy, and a friend in his early manhood, has been called, for his poems in the dialect, " the true poet of Wessex life." He pictures Autumn nights in the following lines :

" Now the light o' the west is a-turn'd to gloom,
    An' the men be at hwome vrom ground ;
    An' the bells be a-zenden all down the Coombe,
    From tower, their mwoansome sound.
    An' the wind is still,
    An' the house-dogs do bark,
    An' the rooks be a-vled to the elems high an' dark
    An' the water do roar at mill."

The sea, too, which now surges along the Wessex coast o'nights with a dirge for the summer that has gone, has taken on its autumn hues. Now at dawn it is grey as a Puritan maiden's gown ; at noon, grey-green as chrysoprase ; and at sunset often a slaty blue, omnious of coming storms.

Its voice upon the shore has altered too ; and the listener for its music hears the low booming as of minute guns—the diapason of the sea ; a harsh rattle of the shingle, like music out of tune. Under the moon the sea is sullen and cold ; and the unbroken fairy moon-track of summer has vanished.

But Autumn sees Wessex with a rare beauty both of foliage and of atmosphere ; and Nature tints her clouds at sunset with no niggardly hand. In the Western sky is often a blaze of glory, which seems to give heightened colour to that of woodland glades and hedgerows.

Winter comes in its turn.

And, too, it has its beauties. The dawn breaks red, and flushes the hills for a brief time. And on fine days, along the coast, the erstwhile pale and ghostly chalk cliffs take on a brief and pearl-like beauty.

Along the lanes, now the bare branches form an intricate and sometimes beautiful tracery against the pale, rain-washed winter sky for those who have eyes to see.

From the upland heights one can see fairy-like valleys emerging for a moment from their enveloping mists ; to disclose views of steel-grey streams and rivers threading their way seaward.

In the meadows and in the pools, where the river has overflowed, or formed backwaters around sharp curves in the banks, the birds of winter give the only touch of life.

On the moors beauty is more sombre and impressive than at other seasons of the year. But there is beauty of a type that Hardy so frequently referred to. A beauty that pervades the heart of the wayfarer with an emotion finely tuned to the vast silence of those lonely wastes. These moors form the inevitable background of some of the tragic and impressive scenes in Hardy's novels and poems.

Indeed, in winter, in daylight or in darkness, these illimitable moors are often the abode of mists and tempests. At night becoming as Hardy wrote, " the home of strange phantoms . . . . the hitherto unrecognised original of those wild regions of obscurity, which are vaguely felt to be compassing us about in midnight dreams . . . . and are never thought of after the dream, till revived by scenes like these."

Along the Wessex coast huge waves are surging . . . winter waves ; angry, hungry and sonorous. And in the sea-washed caves there is the booming, organ-note of storm ; carried often miles inland by the rising gale. From the rocks, lashed by the white crests of surges broken in their onslaught upon the immovable, comes the sharper music of a wailing note ; half-wind and half of seething foam.

Winter has touched the sea with its darkling spell, and come are

> " The strong, shouting days and nights that run,
> All white with stars, across the labouring ways
> Of billows warm with storm, instead of sun.
>
> . . . .
>
> And as one stands upon some sea-girt height
> " By some tempestuous bay,
> What time the great sea waxes warm and white
> And beats and blinds the following wind with spray . ."

The watcher feels at last the spell of winter's rude magnificence.

But its most beautiful aspect is when hoar-frost and snow comes, turning the bare into the clothed, with its bridal garment of white ; and its sparkling jewels of rime ; making the hedgerows one fairy-like tracery of sparkling whiteness.

Each blade of grass in the meadow is now a gemmed spear for fairy folk. Brighter, in the winter sunshine, than any polished lance of knight of old. Along the waysides withered thistles and upstanding teasles are transformed into exquisite clusters of sparkling gems and fairy diadems.

On the uplands the gorse is rime-laden and beautiful, with the fretted webs of spiders, like the framework of rose-windows in the shining walls of some fairy palace.

The great moors and Hardy's Egdon Heath, which lies beneath the winter's sun, are glistening with the exquisite sheen of frosted silver, and pools that lay dull under lowering skies, now glint like blinking eyes at the wayfarer. At night becoming steel-like mirrors under the pale-faced moon. Here and there a red-breasted robin " Christ's own bird," carols on a gorse twig, or from the naked branch of some storm-beaten tree. But all other voices of Nature are still.

But there is yet a fairer beauty at times, when on moor, in vale and coppice, and on hillsides white snowflakes have fallen, blotting out all ugly things ; all angles of Nature's architecture.

Then it is a white world indeed that lies under the winter sky.   A world of imagery, shining in the fitful gleams of the winter sun.

Then at even :

" Burning logs, drawn from near-by copse and ancient
          wood,
      Smoulder ruddy on the hearth,
      And the flames send shadows dancing,
      Keeping time to upward-flying sparks.
      While outside the winter wind is voicing
      Dirge-like music of the dying day."

CHAPTER III

DORCHESTER, THE CAPITAL OF HARDY'S WESSEX

O
F ALL THE TOWNS that have played their part in the
history of Wessex in past ages, Dorchester, which may
justly be called the Capital of Hardy's Wessex, is one
of the most important ; none are more interesting.

It is set almost in the centre of South Wessex, surrounded
by meadow land, north, west and east, and is environed by
gradually rising uplands ; sloping towards the coast southward. It owed much of its ancient importance to the fact
that through it passes one of the great Roman roads, the Via
Iceniana or Icknield Street. This great highway of the past
runs south westward from Salisbury to Woodyates, lying
just within the Dorset county border. Thence it passes a
little north of Sturminster Marshall on its way to Athelhampton, where there is Athelhampton House, one of the
most lovely places in Wessex, the greater part dating from the
fifteenth century. The Roman road goes on, straight as a line,
to Dorchester, over hedges and ditches. And at Stinsford
joins the modern motor road.

Doubtless the existence of this great historic highway has
done much to enable Dorchester to retain its importance down
to the present time.

It remains a thriving and picturesque country town ;
perhaps, a trifle quiet, except on market days. Then there is
an air of bustle and commerce in its streets. And, in Hardy's
time it was, as I also knew it, full of the types of Wessex folk
that he so vividly described. Once it was a Roman base, with

homes of nobles, and a garrison of Cæsar's legionaries. And to-day it is of great antiquarian interest by reason of this ; and also because of its position as the centre of a prosperous dairy and sheep-breeding area.

The town is pleasantly situated on rising ground which to the north slopes to the valley of the Frome, and when approached by the Puddletown-Dorchester road, presents a very picturesque appearance across the meadows meeting Fordington, its eastern portion.

Woven into the fabric of its history are stirring events. It has been occupied in turn by Saxons, Romans and Danes ; the latter of whom came in their galleys up the Wareham Channel to within a few miles of Dorchester. Important and sometimes lurid events too, have not been lacking from its history in the past. Fierce battles were fought in its vicinity ; and the town was more than once besieged. It remains proud of its stirring story ; and today presents a good example of an interesting and picturesque Wessex town.

In Roman times Durnovaria, to give it the name it then bore, was the centre of a civilising influence. And beneath the streets lie pavements along which Roman legions marched in triumph ; or took their way, when in search of recreation, to the amphitheatre known as Maumbury Rings, situated near the Railway Station to the south of the town. The origin of this survival has often been disputed ; regarding whether it is British or Roman. But in 1908 and subsequent years considerable excavations were initiated and carried out by Mr. C. S. Prideaux and Mr. H. St. George Gray, and discoveries were made which proved that its origin had to be dated back nearly 2000 years prior to the Roman occupation of Dorchester. As the result of their work it was proved, it is said, without question to have been a Sacred Circle of the Stone Age. It at that period comprised a ditch encircled by a rampart. In the former shafts had been sunk to a depth of some 30ft. to be used for some ritual purpose, and were afterwards filled up. So that the Roman legionaries, when they came found a site ready to serve as an arena.

The " Rings " are oval, and consist of a series of raised mounds, partly enclosing an open space, which is about 218 feet in length by 163 feet in width.

Maumbury too, is one of the most perfect survivals of its kind in Great Britain ; with an estimated seating capacity for from 10,000 to 12,000 spectators at the gladiatorial combats that probably took place in it during the Roman occupation. By some authorities it is considered possible that the dens for the wild beasts taking part in these encounters were situated under the thickest portions of the rows of seats overlooking the arena.

Readers of Hardy's novel *The Mayor of Casterbridge* will remember this is the spot which he selected for the meeting of Michael Henchard, the Mayor, and his wife, Susan, after their long separation. It is around Maumbury Rings that many legends have been woven. Indeed tradition asserts that even in broad daylight people sitting in the arena, on raising their eyes from the book they may possibly be reading, or upon opening them after a doze, have been startled to see the green slopes lined with spectral Roman soldiery, apparently intent on some combat taking place in the arena below them

Even the hoarse murmur of the voices of these long dead Romans is said to be heard, ere the vision vanishes as swiftly as it was conjured up !

For many years, when the sides of Maumbury Rings had become grass-grown, the place was used as one of public execution. And on March 21, 1705, that of Mary Channing, took place. As a mere girl she had been compelled by her parents to marry a Dorchester grocer, Richard Channing. She was in love with some other man ; and her life was dull and loveless so far as she was concerned. In the end she poisoned her husband ; it was said by white mercury. She was tried at the Summer Assizes of 1704, found guilty, and condemned to death by strangling. She was then only nineteen years of age. She was strangled, and afterwards her body was burned. She had been dragged to the place of execution protesting her innocence, and it is said that a crowd of 10,000 people witnessed the horrible scene. In 1767 Maumbury was abandoned as a place of execution, and the gallows site was removed to a spot on Bradford Down, a mile or so along the Dorchester to Bridport road.

Outside Dorchester are other Roman and Saxon remains, both earthworks, with which the early history of the town is closely associated. The first, Poundbury stands a short distance on the western side on elevated ground above the river. In far off days there was a huge lake to the north, a mile wide, connected with the Frome. And on that side it needed only a single rampart to defend the camp. One can enter the enclosure at the north-west corner by a trackway.

Some two miles south of Dorchester lies Mai-Dun, or "Hill of Strength," commonly known as Maiden Castle. It is a solitary spot not far from the Roman Road. About this there has been considerable dispute as to its antiquity. But discoveries made during excavations in 1934, and subsequent years under the direction of Dr. R. E. M. Wheeler, D.Litt. (Lond.), keeper of the London Museum, have established its great antiquity. Including evidences of Neolithic, Early Iron Age, and Belgic and Roman occupation dating back as far as about 2500 to 2000 B.C. Many domestic and other objects of these periods having been discovered. It is situated upon the flat top of a hill, and covers no fewer than 115 acres. The space within the ramparts occupying 45 acres. It was totally abandoned centuries ago, and it taxes one's imagination to conceive how, with the primitive tools available in the age of its construction, the work was ever accomplished.

No doubt, because its original inhabitants absolutely deserted it, and none others came, it remains in perfect preservation, as a monument to the builders, found there by the Romans on their invasion of Britain. The three ramparts forming the defences are some 60 feet in height and very steep, so that to enter the inner portion of the camp is a matter of some difficulty.

Dorchester and its immediate vicinity is indeed, rich in Roman remains. As Hardy wrote " it announces old Rome in every street, alley and precinct. It looked Rome, bespoke the Art of Rome, concealed dead men of Rome. It was impossible to dig more than a foot or two deep about the town, fields and gardens, without coming upon some tall soldier or other of the Empire, who had lain there in his silent, unobtrusive rest for a space of fifteen hundred years."

The town still is on the lines of its Roman builders ; possessing four main thoroughfares, North Square, South Street, High East Street, and High West Street.

Dorchester has always been important from one point of view or another. And in the middle of the eleventh century, in the reign of Edward the Confessor, had no less than 172 houses or dwellings ; and by the reign of Henry VIII the number had grown to 349.

The history of Dorchester like that of other original settlements of the type, has been marked by many stirring events, and its progress through the centuries of its existence has been steady and prosperous.

It was of great strategic importance in Roman times ; was more than once ravaged by the Danish invaders ; received visits from King John which, we are told, were not appreciated ! and also has been the scene of hangings and quarterings ; the burning of a witch ; and was scourged by the plague in 1348 " when the inhabitants suffered much, and died in great numbers."

The most devastating of the several fires that occurred broke out on an August afternoon in 1613, while many of the townsfolk were away from home working in the harvest fields. It started in the house of a tallow chandler, a bad place, because of the inflammable nature of the contents, and spread rapidly. Over 300 houses were destroyed, and only one of the three Churches was saved, that of St. Peter. The other two, Holy Trinity and All Saints', were destroyed. The loss to the inhabitants was disastrous, and a collection was made all over the country for the sufferers. And we are told " one Matthew Chubb, did advance and lay out one thousand pounds to those who had sustained loss, which was to be repaid by the King (James I) the next subsidy following."

In connection with this catastrophe another appeal was made stating that, " as it has pleased God to awaken the inhabitants by this fiery trial," a collection would be made for the purpose of providing a hospital, and a house of correction. The money proved to be forthcoming ; and part of it was used to build a 'brew-house' (brewery), out of the profits from which it was hoped to have funds to carry on the hospital.

Other fires having damaged the town in 1622, 1725 and 1775, the inhabitants were at last aroused to take steps against such incidents, and adopt measures to extinguish them more efficiently when they occurred. It was therefore agreed, we are told, " to provide leather buckets (called ' tankards ') to be hung up in the Church of St. Peter. And a few years later steps were taken to procure " a brazen engine or spouts, to quench fire in the time of danger." That is to say a brass syringe, which had to be held up by two men, and operated by a third !

Dorchester saw something of the Civil War between King Charles and his Parliament, and supported the latter so strongly as to be reckoned by the Royalists as " the seat of great maglignity." In 1642 the town was provided with walls, forts and platforms to enable it to be defended if attacked.

But, on the approach of the King's forces under the Earl of Caernarvon in 1643, after his successful attack upon Bristol, the townsfolk decided to surrender, and after negotiating with the Earl, they delivered up all their arms, and ammunition, and " assured that they should not be plundered nor suffer any ill for what they had done," surrendered the town. But during the ensuing months Dorchester was made to suffer severely at the hands of both parties in the strife ; being taken and re-taken several times ; and had no peace until it was captured by the Earl of Essex, and was thereafter held for the Parliament.

Cromwell himself came in March, 1645, with a large force, amounting to some four thousand men, and a fierce battle took place outside the town between some of the Cromwellian horse, and the troops of General Goring ; who, taking the Parliamentarians in the rear, compelled them to retire across the river into the town.

From this time onward, noted in the reigns of Elizabeth, Charles I and James I for its cloth manufacture, Dorchester went on its quiet undisturbed way, until the coming of the Duke of Monmouth. Some of the townsfolk and the country people round about became involved in the rebellion, which occurred in the West Country.

The unfortunate Duke, a natural son of Charles II and Lucy Walters, landed on June 11, 1685 at Lyme Regis in his tragic endeavour to win a crown. Thousands of the country-folk and some of the nobility flocked to his standard ; but a little less than a month later, on July 6 he was utterly defeated at Sedgemoor, and, after two days of cross country flight, was captured near Wimborne in an enclosure of land, then known as " the island," but now as Woodlands Farm. He was taken before a Magistrate, Anthony Ettrick, and committed for trial. He set out for Ringwood, and was lodged in a house, still known as Monmouth House, on the town side of the ford. Two days later he left for London on horseback, with his hands tied behind him. And seven days later was executed upon Tower Hill.

Dorchester's treasonable connection with the Rebellion, was slight. But the town was visited on September 3 by the infamous Judge George Jeffreys to hold his " Bloody Assize." One learns from an account prepared by " Several West Country Gentlemen, who were both Eye and Ear Witnesses to All matter of Fact " that on the day following the arrival of the Judge " with his Assistants, Gown-men and Sword-men " an " excellent Sermon was preached before their Lordships, by a worthy Divine, Chaplain to a Worthy Person of that County, much tending to Mercy. It was, however, observed that while my Lord Chief Justice was at Church, in Prayers as well as Sermon, he was seen to laugh, which was so unbecoming a person in his Character that ought, in so weighty an affair as he was entering upon, to have been more serious, and have craved the Help and Assistance of God Almighty."[*]

In the most interesting account of the trial which has just been quoted it is made clear that Jeffreys not only tricked many of the accused into pleading guilty on the promise of clemency ; but what was more heinous sent " a couple of officers into the gaol, to call over, and take the names of the Prisoners ; on the promise that if they confest, they might expect mercy ; otherwise not."

Many confessed, and these confessions were devised to ensure that any who pleaded not Guilty could be convicted on the confession, " which so disposed of the remaining great numbers, which put an end to any further trial. The only thing remaining was to pronounce sentence upon them, which were in number 292, who received sentence of Death all at once."

The total number of those presented for trial at the Assizes was 312 of whom 74 were executed, 175 transported to work on the Plantation, 9 fined and or whipped, and 54 discharged.

---

[*]From " The Bloody Assizes ; or the Life of Judge Jefferies. Faithfully collected by Several West Country Gentlemen, who were both Eye and Ear Witnesses to all matter of Fact."

Hangman's Cottage
Dorchester.
"Casterbridge"

In the case of those condemned we are told " they were executed and their Quarters sent up and down the Country to the dread of the Spectators, as well as the annoyance of the Travellers."

Jeffreys grateful sovereign James II, as a reward for his diligence with the Rebels, and work in Dorsetshire and the West Country, made him Lord Chancellor of England.

A remarkable thing concerning him is that his best known and most striking portrait, painted by Sir Godfrey Kneller, who was Court painter, shows not a trace of the hideous character of the most execrated of all remembered English Judges. He is depicted as a man of slight build ; clean-shaven, as was then the fashion ; with a gentle and refined counternance, and rather sleepy eyes.

In justice his end, which came four years after the " Bloody Assize," was as horrible as his life. At forty-five he was sent to the Tower of London, loathsome from disease, hated by the common people of England ; and, as one writer puts it, " when he crossed the drawbridge of his prison, it was to the roar of a great city disappointed of its revenge."

One can still see in Dorchester, a little way up the High West Street on the opposite side of the road to St. Peter's Church, the ancient half-timbered house, with over-hanging upper story, now a Restaurant, where Judge Jeffreys lodged during the " Bloody Assize." From the balcony there was a view of the Gaol. And it is said that the Judge stood upon it to watch the executions of his victims.

In the County Museum is preserved the chair in which the Judge sat during the trial ; and a spike upon which the head of one of the rebels had been affixed after execution.

Dorchester of the past must have been a rather delightful and picturesque town, and has retained those characteristics to the present day. Formerly there were in the vicinity of St. Peter's Church quaint and interesting Flemish houses of plaster and timber. Then the Market-house stood in the centre of the town, and was known as the Cupola, by reason of its dome-like construction. This was pulled down in 1782, as it had become an obstacle to the increasing traffic. In North Square there stood what was known as the ' Blind House,' in which " drunks and disorderlies " of the town were incarcerated for the night.

The town of the past had narrow cobbled streets, with houses crowded together, some of them were with thatched roofs. The inns were very prosperous and numerous in coaching days; with the bustle attendant upon the arrival of the mails and distinguished visitors.

Even the town of Hardy's boyhood and early manhood was very different from that of to-day. Not so much in the buildings, though some have been pulled down, and others altered; but more in the types one sees in the streets and especially on Market Days. The changes, however, have not been so numerous or radical as in many other Wessex towns during a like passing of the years.

But to understand the atmosphere created by Hardy's novels, and the reality of the characters in them, one must at least try to conjure up a picture of Dorchester of the middle half of last century. Now-a-days one seldom sees, as one did half-a-century ago, the ' smocked ' yokels in the streets; and the shepherds do not so often come along them with their flocks, and with dogs barking in their efforts to control the stragglers. Nor do old women appear driving their pigs. And the itinerant scissors-grinder, with his strangely-shaped barrow is less seldom seen; as are also the pedlars with trays of bootlaces, braces, cottons, and gaily coloured ribbons; and the donkeys one used to see, heavily laden with sacks or baskets of fodder.

The market folk, too, though of the same type, and some of whom still speak in the vernacular of William Barnes' poems, seem, somehow to have lost much of the picturesqueness they used to possess. The motor car has displaced the governess car of former times ; the family equipage with its two well-groomed horses has disappeared ; the village doctor's gig, which used to be seen, when he had to come into the town from outlying hamlets for physic or other necessities of his profession is no longer seen ; and one does not often nowadays come across the prosperous farmer in his dogcart.

But Dorchester, has to some extent, retained a pleasant savour of the past, which seldom fails to impress the visitor, and it is still picturesque. It is true that in some measure it has suffered by the ' march of progress,' and at the hands of the speculating builder, and now has, compared with Hardy's day, suburbs ; the architecture of which adds little distinction or attraction to their surroundings.

There was a time indeed, within memory of the older inhabitants, when one seemed to step out of the streets of the town into the countryside, and at that time there was a mill at the end of North Square, by the river. And, if a stranger, one was quite surprised to come upon a cornfield not far beyond the end of South Street. Now part of that area has become industrialised, with a vast Brewery, which was founded in 1837, burned down in 1922, and has now, with railway sidings and great increase in the extent of its buildings, since it was rebuilt, after the last fire, become a prominent feature of the town.

Fordington, or what may be described as the east end of the town, is still one of the least spoiled, and remains one of the most picturesque of its survivals. Hardy gave to it the name of Durnover, a version of the Roman one Durnovaria. From Grey's Bridge, in Hardy's day the gossiping place of idlers on fine evenings, one obtains an attractive view of the lower portion as well as the upper of Fordington, which is dominated by the square tower of its Church. Much of the squalidness of Mill Lane which existed in Hardy's time, has disappeared. In the *Mayor of Casterbridge* he described it as " The Adullum of all the surrounding villages, the hiding-place of those who were in distress, and in debt, and trouble of every kind." Fordington of the past figures in several of his novels and poems, and in his books of short stories.

Down in Fordington, the water meadows, in which cows graze, still lie close to the gardens of some of the houses.

For many years building and development of the town on its north-eastern outskirts was held up by the fact that Fordington Field, some 3,000 acres in extent, was held under an unusual tenure of the Duchy of Cornwall " in farthings or Fourthings (which is a quarter of a hide or ' caracute ') from which the field derived its original name of " Fourthington."

It may be explained that a ' hide ' of land is a piece, variously estimated, that could be ploughed by one plough in a year, and was considered capable of maintaining a family. The restrictions arising out of this tenure were abolished some years ago.

It is interesting to note that the land in Dorchester, held under the Duchy of Cornwall, extended to the site of Hardy's home at " Max Gate," and therefore belonged to the Prince of Wales of that time, now known as the Duke of Windsor. Hardy became the first freeholder under the Crown for many generations ; and had been granted to him, one may imagine, as a special concession by reason of his eminence in Literature.

On July 30, 1924, the then Prince of Wales, paid Hardy a visit, and had lunch at " Max Gate." His Royal Highness was on a tour of the West Country to visit portions of the Duchy of Cornwall Estates.

One was told afterwards how pleased Hardy was, how much he appreciated the visit ; and the unconventional conversation he had with the Prince.

Not the least charm of Dorchester is the fact that it is encircled by what are known as Walks. They are four in number, the South Walks, West Walks, Bowling Alley Walks and Colliton Walks ; and are leafy promenades or boulevards which were constructed and planted on the sites of the old town walls at the time the latter were demolished. On three sides the town is now surrounded by these delightful avenues, which date from between the years 1700 and 1712, and on the fourth side by the Frome. These avenues give Dorchester a distinctive and pleasing character, reminding one not a little of some Continental towns.

" Max Gate," Hardy's home from Midsummer, 1885 until he died January 11, 1928, stands about a mile outside the town. It is surrounded by a considerable garden and trees, and is of villa type of the period to which it belongs, erected from Hardy's own designs. During his lifetime it was one of the ' show ' places in Dorset. People from all parts, even from abroad and the United States, used to go out of the town to see it, with the hope of catching a glimpse of its world-famed owner. And during the holiday and tourist season, in fine weather, it was seldom that people were not found outside the gate.

In the early days the house door could be seen from the road ; but the trees, many of them Austrian pines, Hardy planted in 1883, soon grew up, and in later years screened the house from the road. It is not too much to say that casual visitors were seldom, if indeed, ever admitted. And after his death sightseers became less and less frequent.

It is now let and the National Trust is concerning itself as regards satisfactory upkeep, and treatment.

But to his birthplace, under the shadow of Edgon Heath, and close to the Memorial which was given by American admirers of his genius, unveiled on April 16th, 1931 by Professor J. Livingstone Lowes of Harvard and Oxford universities, each year numbers of people make pilgrimage in the holiday season. The thatched cottage, amid such surroundings as the great Heath, provides a scene well in keeping with Hardy's origin, his love of Nature and his great achievement.

THOMAS HARDY O.M.
WAS BORN IN MEMORY
COTTAGE 2ND JUNE 1840
AND HE WROTE
UNDER AN ADJOINING TREE
ADD
THE FIRST FEW CHAPTERS

THIS MONUMENT ERECTED
HIS FRIENDS AND FELLOW
HIS AMERICAN ADMIRERS
1931

THE AMERICAN MEMORIAL
TO THOMAS HARDY. 1931

Douglas SNOWDON

UPPER BOCKHAMPTON.
(Egdon Heath.)

The memorial is of classic simplicity. A monolith of rough-hewn Cornish granite, and on it hang bronze laurel wreaths. The inscription reads as follows :—

THOMAS HARDY, O.M.
was born in the adjacent cottage
2nd June, 1840
and in it wrote "Under the Greenwood Tree"
and "Far from the Madding Crowd."
This monument is erected to his memory by a few of
his American admirers, 1931.

The Birthplace, still a thatched cottage-like building, though less in extent, and in other ways altered from what it was when Hardy was born there, "is weatherworn and reduced." Once there were belonging to the house two gardens, a portion of one of which was orchard ; a horse paddock ; also stabling and other buildings, and from the inside the wide chimney-corner, so often a striking feature of a sitting room, in such a dwelling, has disappeared.

In an early poem Hardy thus himself describes his home and its surroundings :—

"It faces west, and round the back and sides
    High beeches, bending, hang a veil of boughs,
    And sweep against the roof.   Wild honeysucks
Climb on the walls, and seem to sprout a wish
(If we may fancy wish of trees and plants)
To overtop the apple-trees hard by.

.   .   .   .

Behind, the scene is wilder.   Heath and furze
Are everything that seems to grow and thrive
Upon the uneven ground.   A stunted thorn
Stands here and there, indeed ; and from a pit
An oak uprises, springing from a seed
Dropped by some bird a hundred years ago."

A picture in words that brings the cottage of half-a-century or so ago to the writer's mind, when he first saw where Hardy was born.

In South Street, with its admixture of architecture and interesting ancient survivals, is the Old Grammar School, now offices and shops ; and Napier's Almhouses, and further up one finds a survival from Tudor times in an archway worth notice.

The Old Grammar School was closed some years ago, and transferred to a new building within sight of " Max Gate," just outside the town. Of which, on July 21, 1927 Hardy laid the founation stone. The crest of the original Thomas Hardy, who founded the school in 1569, was a wyvern's head, an interesting fact in this connection is that, after more than three centuries, the crest is worn on the cricket caps of the scholars.

The original school had many vicissitudes, it was burned down in the great fire of 1613, rebuilt five years later and pulled down in 1879 ; but through all the happenings there is a stone in the wall of the first school bearing the arms of Queen Elizabeth and the date 1569.

In past times Dorchester has been well served by its citizens, and not least by those who concerned themselves chiefly with the welfare and happiness of their fellow townsfolk.

There were three sets of Almshouses erected by private charity. The first, built and founded by Matthew Chubb, who was Member of Parliament for Dorchester, in 1602, the first year of the reign of James I ; and by Margaret his wife. The second were given by John Wetstone, who in 1614 left in his Will £500 to the town for that purpose.

The third foundation was that of Napper's Mite, or Napper's Almshouse situated on the eastern side of South Street, next door to the old Grammar School ; it is a stone building with a projecting clock, and a delightful cloister. It was founded in 1615 for the accommodation of ten poor men, by Sir Robert Napper, or Napier, of Middlemarch. In connection with this charity, a succeeding baronet, Sir Gerard Napper, left by Will, in 1667, all his Manor of Stert, in the Parish of Babcary Somerset, for the purpose of providing a divine service once a day, to his alms-people in Dorchester, and, for catechising them once a week ; £5 to either the schoolmaster of Dorchester for the time being or his usher ; and, after payment of the said £5, to set apart so much of the rents and profits of the said Manor as, together with the yearly profits of the chambers of his almshouse, would make and provide convenient gowns for the alms-people of the said almshouse once in two years." The remainder of the profits of the said manor were to be equally divided amongst the alms-people.

On the opposite side of the street is the house once occupied by William Barnes, the poet of Wessex, when he kept a school in the town.

The Town Memorial Statue to Hardy is in the Colliton Walks on the grass verge, situated where High West Street and the Grove meet. It is an impressive life-size statue showing him seated in meditative mood with his hat on his knees. The inscription on the base is as follows. "THOMAS HARDY, 1840-1928." There is a bronze laurel leaf wreath below it. The statue was unveiled on September 2nd, 1931 by his friend Sir James Matthew Barrie, O.M. in the presence of a distinguished company.

At the top of South Street stands St. Peter's Church, the chief ecclesiastical feature of Dorchester today, which once possessed a number of churches, and now only St. Peter's, All Saints and Holy Trinity. The first named is thought to have been erected on the site of a Roman Temple, and is of great antiquity. Outside is the striking statue of the Rev. William Barnes, the friend of Hardy, and an acknowledged poet in the Dorset dialect.

The Church is a fine building in the Perpendicular style, with traces of surviving Saxon work, and with an early Norman porch. The handsome tower, 90 ft. in height, is a well-known landmark. The building contains a number of interesting monuments, among them effigies supposed to be those of the Chideock family, at the time of the Dissolution of the Monasteries, removed from the Priory which stood hard by. One of the quaintest of the memorials is that to the famous Denzil Holles, who was one of the members of the House of Commons who held the Speaker Finch down in his chair until Parliament had passed its famous Resolution in 1639 ; and who was also one of the five members Charles I accused of high Treason, and attempted to arrest in 1642. Holles's effigy is seen reclining on a cushion, dressed in the costume of an ancient Roman. There is an amusing anachromism in his feet being shod with Roman sandles, while he wears a full bottomed wig ! His attendants are some remarkably fat weeping cherubs.

The Church possesses a fine Jacobean pulpit ; and an interesting rood staircase. There is also a monument to the Thomas Hardy who founded the Grammar School ; and a fine and very ancient brass to Johanna St. Omero the widow of Robert More, who died in 1436, should be noted.

The south aisle, which is embattled, and has its eastern end raised, is of very notable architecture ; much of it being fifteenth century work. And the south door should be noted by students and those interested in architecture, as it is a rather curious example of Transition-Norman, with an arch pointed and richly ornamented with mouldings of purely Norman character ; the jambs are chamfered, and the rich mouldings are stopped by small carved brackets of an Early English type.

Of the other two Churches little need be said. All Saints' stands in High East Street, and is an elegant building, with a striking and lofty spire, built in the first half of the last century. The west window is a memorial to Mr. Troyte, who did much of the work with his own hands. Under the tower is an interesting altar-tomb to Matthew Chubb, who died in 1625, which was taken from the old church.

The remaining Church of Holy Trinity, is a modern Gothic building, rebuilt in 1824, which does not call for any particular attention or description.

Fordington Church, lying just outside the town boundary, was originally in the Transition-Norman style, and cruciform in plan. It has, unfortunately, suffered rather badly at the hands of restorers. But it is still worth visiting and study from the fact of its preserving several features of considerable interest to architectural students and archæologists. The impressive tower is of the type of those often found in Somersetshire. There is a very interesting flat bas-relief, representing a vision of St. George, to whom the Church is dedicated. It is to be seen on the tympanum of the south door, near which is also a holy-water stoup of unusual type. The stone pulpit, bearing the date of 1592 E.R. is worth notice.

Among other 'objects of interest' in Dorchester is the County Gaol, built on the ground formerly occupied by the ancient castle. It stands on the rising ground to the north side of the town, and it contains a very unusual feature in such a building, the tessellated pavement of the chapel. This is a Roman one, some twenty feet square, re-laid after discovery with other antiquities in 1858, when a grave was being dug for the reception of a murderer.

Of the ancient Priory little more than the name remains, although it was undoubtedly once the most important foundation of the Franciscan Order in the County.

The old County Hall, in High West Street, is unimpressive built at the time when 'Bonnie Prince Charlie,' the Young Pretender was giving the Governmen anxiety. And setting afloat disturbing rumours by his march into England during his unsuccessful, but romantic endeavour, to wrest the crown from George II.

The New County Hall is situated in Colliton Park, Dorchester, being the administrative centre of the County. The building occupies a site of some 10 acres, which is said not to have been built upon since the Roman occupation. It contains accommodation for all Administrative Departments, Council Chambers, Crown Court, Committee Rooms, and rooms for other Public purposes. This foundation stone was laid by the Right Hon. The Earl of Shaftesbury, H.M. Lord Lieutenant for the County of Dorset, on September 26th, 1938.

The Town Hall, standing hard-by St. Peter's Church, has an effective open-timbered roof, and here is to be seen the chair used by Judge Jeffreys when at Dorchester during his "Bloody Assize." Though its authenticity is questioned by some authorities, and it was supposed to have been lost at one period, tradition states that it is genuine.

The County Museum which stands at the side of St. Peter's Church, possesses one of the most interesting archæological collections in the country. It also contains a considerable number of Town records of great interest ; and some of a distinctly humourous character. The collection of British and Roman antiquities, found during various works of excavation and building operations in the town and neighbourhood, is a very fine one, and well worth study and close examination by students and visitors. There is also a good collection of local fossils found in the beds at Kimmeridge and the Isle of Purbeck.

Those interested in old survivals will find a most horrible collection of man-traps and sets of 'stocks' for both feet and hands. Also examples of the reeve stocks or staves, used in former times for recording, by means of notches cut in them, the tenures of land. And there is a halberd blade, which had been converted into a sword by a smuggler, who was captured at Preston, during a run of contraband goods as late as 1835. Among other curious things, likely to interest the musically minded, is what was called a " humstrum," or old Dorset Viol, which has long passed out of use. William Barnes wrote of it's passing, somewhat in sorrow, though, from all accounts, it was a " passing poor " instrument. His lines are as follows :

" But now a bow do never screape
   A humstrum anywhere around,
 An' zome can't tell a humstrum's sheape,
   An' never heard his jinglen sound."

There are also in the Museum two horrible looking leaden weights, made to the order of a humanely disposed governor of the gaol, to be tied to the feet of a man when he was hanged for committing arson in 1836. On the weights are the words MERCY, and they were made because the governor thought the man was so light that he would not get his neck broken by the drop ; but hang strangling.

There is also a handsome bell-ringer's pewter flagon. After a visit on one New Year's Eve to the belfrey, Hardy made an entry in his diary as follows : " To St. Peter's belfrey to the New Year's Eve ringing. The night wind whiffed in through the louvres as the men prepared the mufflers with tar twine and pieces of horse-cloth. Climbed over the bells to fix the mufflers. I climbed with them, and looked into the tenor bell ; it is worn into a bright pit, where the clapper has struck it for so many years, and the clapper is battered with its many blows . . . . .

" The grey stones of the fifteenth century masonry have many of their joints mortarless, and are carved with many initials and dates. On the sill of one louvred window stands a great pewter pot with a hinged cover and engraved " For the use of the ringers 1626."

As ever, Hardy was the keenest of observers, and one of the greatest of note takers. The tankard mentioned is that now in the County Museum.

One of the most interesting features in the Museum is a reconstruction of Hardy's Study, as it was at " Max Gate,"

Stinsford Church. "Mellstock"

with his writing table, chair, and other furniture, and many of his books and pictures. This " room " never fails to interest visitors.

From outside the Museum is obtained one of the most comprehensive and satisfying views of the town, the road sloping eastward down to the river and water meadows. On either side of it are a line of shops and houses of irregular, and therefore of a pleasing character. Scarcely two alike. There are some of the bow-windows of a more dignified age than the present ; and here and there still a stone portico. And the shops in summer give a touch of colour with their sun blinds. The road runs on its way across the Gray's Bridge in the water meadows till it disappears amid the trees of Stinsford.

Many people have of recent years visited the little village, which is the West Mellstock of Hardy's novels and poems, and is described in and is the scene of incidents in *The Mayor of Casterbridge, Tess of the D'Urbervilles, Under the Greenwood Tree*, and the poem *The Dead Quire*. The village is but a mile or so from the outskirts of Dorchester. The church is an Early English building, with a good Perpendicular South Aisle, and has a marble and Caen stone reredos, and a white marble font. On the face of the tower is a bas-relief of St. Michael. In this church Hardy was christened, and the family worshipped, and several of the older generation of Hardys played instruments in the choir.

In this little Church, which is most visited because of Hardy's association with it, there is a fine stained-glass window the subject of which is the prophet Elizah, and incidents recorded in I. Kings, chap. 19, verses 11 and 12.

The Inscription is as follows :—

" To the glory of God and in memory of Thomas Hardy, O.M. 1840-1928. Poet and Novelist, born in this village, where his heart lies buried. This window is given by public subscription."

The memorial organ was the gift of Katherine Hardy, sister of the novelist, in memory of her parents and her brothers and sisters.

It was in the tree-surrounded churchyard, and the shadow of a great yew tree, that, on January 16, 1928 Hardy's heart in a casket was buried in the grave of his first wife, among the family graves, and in the presence of so many he had known and who had known him.

To have been buried there had been his wish. But it was thought more seemly to do him honour by burial in Westminster Abbey. So there his ashes repose, while his heart rests in the Wessex that he loved so well.

CHAPTER IV

SOME PLEASANT AND PICTURESQUE TOWNS

THERE ARE MANY interesting little towns in Hardy's Wessex as well as some larger ones. Not all of them figure to any great degree in his novels and poems, and this is the case with Wimborne. It is interesting in itself and historically important, and, although mentioned in *Two on a Tower* and is the scene of a short story in *A Group of Noble Dames*, is referred to for those two foregoing reasons rather than for having a close association with the novel mentioned.

Wimborne, or as Hardy calls it Warborne, had considerable importance in former days because of its ecclesiastical status, which prestige was lost on the suppression, and in many cases the destruction, of the Monastic and other Religious foundations. Nowadays its chief life is still rather more rural than urban ; and somewhat similar to the placid course of the two streams, the Allen or Wim and Stour, on which it stands. It is a picturesque and pleasant valley through which they flow on their way to Christchurch and the sea.

The history of Wimborne has been in past ages less stirring than that of some Wessex towns of similar importance. Although in times of Anglo-Saxon invasion it doubtless knew and heard of the great battle, fought about A.D. 520, which raged about three and a half miles from the town at Badbury Rings, between the Britons under King Arthur, and the Anglo-Saxons under Cedric.

Wimborne was disturbed by war some four centuries later, when Ethelbald seized the town. He was a cousin of

Edward the Elder, who promptly marched against him ; and, in strong force, encamped at Badbury Rings. On the King's approach the rebels fled, and joined the Danes in Northumberland. Though these two events may be held to constitute Wimborne's stirring early history, it is known to have been a place of importance and of considerable size in Roman times, and that it became a military station bearing the name of Vindogladia.

Early in the days of the introduction of Christianity it became famous on account of the nunnery founded there about A.D. 700 by Cuthberga ; a sister of Ina, King of Wessex.

There is a charming view of the town, with the red sandstone towers of its ancient Minster rising amidst the picturesque roofs of the older houses, obtained from the bridge over the river and across the water meadows. As one enters the town from the south one cannot fail to realise its old-world charm, although, of course, it has altered in some particulars from what it was when Hardy lived there from 1881 onwards at a villa called " Llanherne," situated in the Avenue.

It is for its fine Church, which possesses several interesting features, and objects of interest connected with it, that the town is generally visited. Fortunately, at the Dissolution of the Monasteries by Henry VIII it was little damaged, and remains a remarkable specimen of a Church in which one finds excellent examples of Norman, Transition-Norman, Early English, and Decorated architecture. In the reign of Elizabeth a foundation, consisting of three priests, with a number of " singing men" and choristers, was instituted, which continues to the present time.

This beautiful old building has during the passing of centuries served the double purpose of a Collegiate and parochial church, and is both interesting and impressive. The two towers, the earlier one, at the intersection of the cruciform, of Transition-Norman date, and the latter, at the western end of the nave, of the Perpendicular period, have a picturesque appearance from almost any point of view. Indeed, many who come to the Minster are for the moment disappointed regarding its size, by reason of the first impression made by its striking towers.

Little nowadays remains of the original fabric except the lantern arches, the piers of the nave, and the walls of the transept and choir. The central tower, with a beautiful open lantern, was once adorned by a spire, by one of the old chroniclers said to have been " as high as that of Salisburie." But there is no surviving evidence of this in the shape of drawings. It had a spire, however, which is generally supposed to have been perhaps some hundred and thirty or even fifty feet in height, which was destroyed by a great storm in 1600 during a service.

In this beautiful and ancient building, picturesque without and within, speaking of so many centuries of worship, one feels that it is truly symbolical of dark ages. But nevertheless speaks to one of high traditions of minstrels, tournaments, crusades and the days of mail-clad chivalry. And that, when in it, we are standing in a place that has known much history.

There are interesting records of this. Near the altar, with a monumental brass let into the pavement to mark the spot, lies royal dust, that of Ethelred, brother of Alfred the Great. He was afterwards canonised, by the Pope of the time and he was, according to most authorities, killed in battle with the Danes, which took place at Marten, Wilts, some fifteen miles North East of Wimborne ; to which town he was afterwards brought for burial. Another king is stated by the Anglo-Saxon Chronicle also to have been buried here in A.D. 962, for it is recorded that " King Sigferth killed himself, and his body lies at Wimborne."

There is a fine altar-tomb, on the south side of the Choir, to John Beaufort, Duke of Somerset and of Margaret Beauchamp, his wife, who died in 1444. He was a grandson of John of Gaunt.

In the south choir aisle is a huge and interesting oak chest, hewn out of a log about seven feet in length. It was formerly used as a safe for the Church plate, records, deeds, etc., and had six locks. It is believed to be at least eleven hundred years old ; and the most ancient chest of its kind in England.

A tomb that has a romantic story attached to it is that of the magistrate Anthony Ettrick, first Recorder of Poole, who committed the Duke of Monmouth after he was captured at Shag Heath. By that act he appears to have become so unpopular with the countryfolk of the district, that, in disgust, he decided he would be buried " neither in nor outside the church, and neither above nor below ground." So an opening was made in the wall on a level with the pavement, and in 1691, which he appears to have believed would be the date of his death, he deposited a black slate or marble coffin in the cavity, on which the date was cut. He did not, however, die until eleven years after !

The quaint old Orrery, connected with the clock, in the west tower, is believed to be almost unique, and was made by one Peter Lightfoot, a Glastonbury monk, in 1320. It has, by means of its mechanism, continued to record the age and phases of the moon, the revolutions of the planets, and the position of the sun according to the Copernican system.

Wimborne Minster possesses what must be reckoned as one of the first Free Libraries to be founded in the South of England. This is a unique collection of chained books, 240 in number, which were collected together by William Stone, one of the clergy attached to the church, a native of the town. It was open to the use of the townsfolk, and, lest the borrowers should take out the books and not return them they were all chained. They are housed in a room reached through the vestry. There are among them several works of note, including the first editions of Sir Walter Raleigh's *History of the World ;* and Burton's *Anatomy of Melancholy.* Among the oldest books are a Latin MS on vellum, *Regimem Animarum,* dated 1343, intended for the use of the priests at that time in the then existing monastery ; and the works of Anselm, printed in 1485.

Over Sir Walter Raleigh's work the poet Prior, who is generally believed to have been a native of the town, is said to have dozed when reading the volume by candlelight, with the result that some hundred leaves were burned through. The damage was, however, repaired as far as possible, by the insertion of discs of paper on which the missing words were written.

The Grammar School is a very ancient foundation, dating from the time of Margaret, Countess of Richmond. It was re-founded by Queen Elizabeth who directed that it should be known as " The Grammar School of the Foundation of Queen Elizabeth in Wimborne Minster." Of these ancient buildings no trace remains. The present School though picturesquely situated, is modern and of no architectural interest. It may be remembered by readers of Hardy that under the disguise of Warborne Grammar School it figures in his novel *Two on a Tower* as the school at which Swithin St. Cleeve was educated. The old school has not, however, been lacking from time to time in scholars of distinction.

Four miles or so of pleasant road will take the pilgrim in Wessex from Wimborne to Poole, across a stretch of heather and gorse-clad moorland, in places almost Scotch in character, though less bleak and impressive than the famous Egdon Heath of the novels, in the region of Bere Regis.

Travellers approaching Poole along the upland road from Wimborne come to a point where it begins to dip down, opening up before them a prospect of almost unrivalled loveliness and charm, embracing the beautiful Harbour stretched out below one, backed to the south-westward by the range of the Purbeck Hills. Away to the eastward, towards Bournemouth, there lies an area of pine woods broken up by the tiny hills of Parkstone ; with fine stretches of the upper reaches of the Harbour, and of the Wareham Channel, and vistas of Poole itself, of Lytchett Heath and the waters of Holes Bay.

Poole, from this vantage point, possesses a picturesqueness conferred on many irregularly built congeries of houses standing near water. One does not see, at this distance, any eyesores that may exist in a small seaport, but only the mass of irregular buildings often wreathed in smoke, and lit on a summer's evening by softening light from the west.

Poole and its harbour have in certain states of the atmosphere an extraordinary and almost eerie beauty, long known to many artists, and acclaimed by several great ones.

The town, Hardy calls it by the apt name of Havenpool, is one of the most ancient of South of England ports ; and more than once in olden days has been on the way to a higher status than it has actually ever attained.

Poole undoubtedly existed early in the history of Wessex, even though one cannot trace it in either Anglo-Saxon or Norman records or Chronicles. It probably had its origin in a lakeside village ; or a settlement on a tongue of land which jutted out into the harbour. But one does find some mention of its existence in a Charter of William Longspée, and we know that in the reign of Henry III in the 13th century, an embargo was put upon all vessels in the port, which seems to point to it being a place of some consequence at the time.

Several historians advance evidence that Poole was originally used as a harbour of refuge, and also as a base for invading operations by the Danes, who several times wintered at Wareham, further up the channel.

About 1341 Poole sent one of its leading men to a Naval Conference held by order of King Edward III. Evidence that even in those days the town had some reputation as a ship-building place. Five years later it was made a garrison town ; and a year or two afterwards furnished four ships manned and armed, with the necessary crews, to form part of the fleet sent to the seige of Calais.

At the beginning of the 15th century there lived in Poole a certain Harry Page (or Paye) who became a famous buccaneer ; often descending in raids on the coast of Spain. And in 1406 a Spanish retaliatory squadron attacked Poole, and later, as a consequence, town walls were built as a defence.

From this time onwards the trade of the town seems to have grown steadily, and the granting of a Royal Charter of Incorporation by Henry VI placed it on a footing of greater importance. During the reign of Elizabeth it was made a County Borough ; a distinction it still retains. During the Civil War, as were other Dorset towns, Poole was held stoutly for the Parliament. As a consequence of this, on the accession of Charles II, the strong walls and fortifications were razed to the ground, of which the postern of the time of Richard III, is almost the only remaining relic.

The chief trade of the port in early times appears to have been of a more or less general character. In more modern times it became that of timber from the Baltic ports. The shipbuilding industry, once important, gradually declined, In the early days of the Newfoundland fisheries there was a considerable trade with them.

The romantic side of Poole's history in the late eighteenth and first half of the nineteenth century, is chiefly concerned with the activities of the most noted and desperate smugglers of the South Coast. The sandy beaches of Studland and Bournemouth ; the wooded chines running far inland, and the creeks of Poole harbour itself, afforded admirable facilities for smuggling, along the very thinly populated coast line of those days.

In 1747, in the night and early morning of 6th-7th October, a band of notorious smugglers, led by one John Diamond, coming from the County of Sussex, numbering between sixty and seventy men "armed to the teeth, and many of them mounted," made an attack upon, and broke into the Custom House on Poole Quay. In the end they carried off 4,000 lbs. of tobacco, many chests of tea and other goods, which had recently been captured from the smugglers by the Customs officers. The smugglers belonged to the notorious Hawkhurst gang, which had become the terror of the countryside ; mentioned in G. P. R. James' novel *The Smuggler*. The Custom House attacked by the smugglers was destroyed by fire in 1815. The present building only dates from the same year.

After seizing the goods the smugglers set out to return to Sussex. They went via Fordingbridge, at which place a number of the inhabitants came out to see them pass. Amongst them was a man Daniel Chater who knew and recognised Diamond.

The event at Poole created a great sensation, and a substantial reward was offered for " information leading to the apprehension and arrest of the chief smugglers." Daniel Chater eventually got into touch with a Collector of Customs, at Southampton, named Shearer. And it was arranged that Chater, as he could identify some of the smugglers, should go with a William Galley, a Customs House officer, carrying a letter to a Major Battin, Justice of the Peace, who was to en-quire of Chater what he knew about the affair and ascertain whether he would be able to identify John Diamond, the ring-leader of the smugglers and others. The smugglers, through informants, were made aware of the objects of the journey, of Daniel Chater and William Galley.

On the two men reaching the White Hart Inn, at Row-land's Castle, they unfortunately fell in with some of the gang of smugglers, who ill-treated them and finally decided to murder them so as to prevent their going on to see Major Battin and give information.

In the end, after suffering horrible cruelties, William Galley was brought to a sandpit, not far from Rake, at a place called Harding Coombe, and, it is said, while still alive was thrown into a grave the smugglers had dug, and there buried.

The unfortunate Daniel Chater, half-dead from the tortures he had suffered, was in the end taken to a disused well in Lady Holt Park, and there half-strangled and thrown into the well. The smugglers casting down stones and earth upon him to prevent the discovery of the crime.

A number of the smugglers were eventually apprehended and brought to trial at Chichester, on January 16th, 1748. The seven charged were tried, convicted and sentenced to death by hanging, and their bodies were hung in chains on gibbets at various places in Sussex.

And thus ended one of the most tragic and horrible crimes committed in connection with smuggling in Wessex.

Smuggling, however, went on vigorously, at first and then less so, along the Sussex, Hampshire and Dorset coasts until the middle half of last century. And the writer's father remembered seeing one Sunday morning a noted Bournemouth smuggler, in the 1850's, galloping down, what is now known as Commercial Road, or Poole Hill, pursued by mounted Customs officers (called riding officers), and soldiers summoned from the Barracks at Christchurch. Poole Road was in those days only a country road, bordered in places with hedges and turf banks, and crossing a tract of moorland stretching from above Parkstone to the outskirts of Bournemouth.

A more agreeable historical memory connected with Poole is the fact that the famous vessel of the Pilgrim Fathers, the *Mayflower*, put in at the port in August 1620 for some repairs, on her way to Plymouth, from whence she set sail for the New World on September 6.

Modern Poole is a very different place to what it was when Hardy wrote the two novels, now more than fifty years ago, in which the town is mentioned ; and the short story *To Please his Wife*, the scene of which is laid in Poole.

In the last War it became a place of considerable importance in several ways. Nowadays there has been marked expansion of its general trade ; and the Town Council have embarked upon a policy of encouraging industrial development in various directions, and with success. The channel leading to the port has been considerably deepened of late years, so that vessels of about 3,000 tons and drawing 16 feet can come to it.

Among the chief trades and industries are ship building, carried on since very early days, and repairs to vessels, pottery, tile making, engineering both light and heavy, timber trade, building industry, foundries, chemical works, toy factories, and fishing, another ancient industry of the port.

Indeed, Poole has greatly grown of recent years chiefly owing to the building of residences at Parkstone, and in the Canford Cliff area, overlooking the harbour. And by extension of business premises.

At Poole we are on the very eastern edge of Hardy's Wessex. Historically it is a rich corner for the readers and admirers of his novels.

In the hollow of the beautiful and impressive Purbeck Hills stands Corfe Castle, one of the finest ruins of its kind in this part of Southern England. It appears, as Corvsgate Castle in two of Hardy's lesser known novels *The Hand of Ethelberta*, and *Desperate Remedies*, as does the village it dominates. And not far away lies quaint and attractive Swanage, called by Hardy, Knollsea, encircling a charming sickle-shape bay, with pleasant downs, and its mill-pond and picturesque stone-roofed cottages well-known to artists.

Corfe Castle stands on a mound between two green hills ; the one to the south-east being the end of Ballard Down, from which are magnificent sea views, also of the countryside and reaches of Poole Harbour.

Corfe village, itself, has an old world air, with its two streets and tiny market-place, in which there is a restored Market Cross ; on the steps of which, at its base, gossips sit and chat. But it is to see its famous castle that most people

Corfe Castle "Corvesgate"

come, which is surrounded by the ruins of its massive stone walls which were, with the castle itself, destroyed by blasting at the order of the Parliamentary leaders in 1646.

The exact date of the Castle is not known, but it is popularly supposed to date from the reign of King Edgar (957-975) ; but, if this be so, there are no defined traces of any Saxon building. The first authenticated historical incident in connection with the castle is that of the assassination of the boy-king Edward, afterwards known as " The Martyr " treacherously stabbed by his stepmother Queen Elfrida, while he was drinking a stirrup cup at the gate. The boy-king rode away, and falling off his horse, was found terribly wounded by the roadside by retainers sent in search.

It is generally held that the original castle was destroyed by Danish invaders in the succeeding reign ; and was not rebuilt till the time of William the Conqueror. It was made a Royal residence in the reign of King John ; and the Crown Regalia was deposited there, during the King's Wars with the Barons.

But it has been a prison as well as a palace ; and two royal prisoners were confined in its gloomy dungeons. Edward II (1327) and Richard II son of the Black Prince (1399). The first was afterwards murdered at Berkeley Castle, and the second at Pomfret Castle.

During the Civil War between Charles I and his Parliament, it was one of the last Royalist strongholds to yield to the Parliament. It had been gallantly and successfully held for some considerable time by Lady Bankes, in the absence of her husband. It was, indeed, not until 1646, after three unsuccessful attempts to take it had been made by the Parliamentary forces, that it was captured through treachery of one of the garrison. It was looted, and then utterly destroyed ; and the magnificent fortress was left a heap of ruined towers, overthrown walls and tottering masonry.

Since then Corfe has had no history. But the curfew bell, upholding an ancient custom, is still rung at Corfe church nightly.

Wareham, which lies at the top of Poole harbour, on the western side, set about a mile from the water, and standing on the little River Frome, is of course, the Anglebury of several of Hardy's novels, especially mentioned in *The Return of the Native* and *The Hand of Ethelberta*.

It is an old-fashioned little town of considerable historical and archæological interest. And possesses a well-preserved Saxon Church of St. Martin, not, however, now used for worship, on the left at the entry to the town on its northern side. Wareham also has remains of earthwork fortifications, and town walls; which from the extent of the latter one judges the place to have formerly been of a greater size.

Like so many Wessex towns, in 1762 it was almost destroyed by fire; and few of its buildings date earlier than the third quarter of the 18th century.

But Wareham was in early times a place of considerable importance, and is mentioned in several Saxon Chronicles and was plundered by the Danes, notably in 876-7. On one occasion they are said by the Saxon Chronicle to have held the town for fifteen months; only abandoning it to march on Exeter.

In the days of Stephen, and during the strife between the King and the Empress Maud, who, as daughter of Henry I, had a good right to the throne, the town suffered severely, and at this period, strange as it may seem today, was reckoned as a port.

In the south-west portion is a site, said to mark the place where stood a castle built by William the Conqueror, which was possibly destroyed in the reign of John.

The Quay, a busy spot no doubt when the town did trade on a large scale with the outside world, is dignified by a square. Alongside the Quay stands the fine Church of St. Mary. It is so close to the River Frome, which runs along the south side of the town, that its handsome tower is reflected in the water. The church possesses an unusually fine organ, and is a most interesting building. There is much worth notice in addition to the usual stone coffins, and crosslegged knights in no longer shining armour. There are several ' puzzle ' inscriptions carved on the walls, which no one seems able to decipher ; and the Norman six-sided leaden font has a little Apostle figure on each of its sides. The claim for the altar to be of Roman origin seems a doubtful supposition. There is also shown a cresset stone, or lamp, bored for five wicks, which floated on oil. It is obviously ancient ; and may, perhaps, have been used by the monks of long ago to light them through the cloisters from the Priory when going to the church for a midnight Mass.

Of great interest to archæologists is the stone with a Danish inscription, serving to remind one that the Danes once held the town. There is also of great interest the St. Edward's Chapel, built about the reign of Henry III to reproduce the one of wood in which the body of Edward the Martyr, killed at Corfe Castle, is said to have been placed. There is, also, a memorial to the Rev. John Hutchins, the author of the well-known and extensive *History of Dorset*.

The Almshouse, with its stone slab roof, and little windows, was endowed in 1418 ; and, as a tablet on its wall tells us, was " founded time immemorial, for six ancient men and five women."

Once the old town possessed no less than eight churches ; but of these only three remain. One is now used as a school ; the other two are St. Martin's, and St. Mary's before referred to and described.

Along the coast is delightful Lulworth Cove, called by Hardy Lulstead Cove, a beauty spot, where Sergeant Troy in *Far from the Madding Crowd* was supposed to have been drowned. It can be reached either by car, or, if a good walker, by way of the pretty Holme Lanes, and Lulworth with its Castle, which was built at the commencement of the seventeenth century. Several kings of England in the olden days stayed there, James I took refuge in it from the Plague ; and Charles II came to it on pleasure bent. And finally George III, when holiday-making in Weymouth as described so vividly in *The Trumpet Major*, paid a visit to the Castle.

The cliffs at the Cove are very lofty, at the highest point 380 ft., and are striking and picturesque. Durdle Door is a section of the chalk cliff pierced right through by the sea so that it forms a natural arch. From the ' look out ' on the summit of a very narrow tongue of land jutting out into the sea, there are fine views along the coastline towards Osmington and Weymouth, and of the not far distant Isle of Portland, " the Isle of Slingers " of Hardy.

At Weymouth, and close adjoining Portland, one steps right into some of the chief scenes of two of Hardy's novels. One the fine, historical romance *The Trumpet Major* so vividly describing the Wessex of the Napoleonic era ; and the other his fantastic story of *The Well-Beloved*.

Weymouth is set chiefly in the western curve of an incomparable Bay, which has been compared by some writers to that of Naples. And has, from the time of George III, progressively developed into the popular and attractive seaside resort of today. It has been well said that the charm of Weymouth Bay is chiefly due to its wide extent, its beautiful curve ; also the varied tints of its environing cliffs ; and the deep blue of its summer sea. To these attractions a wide stretch of level sands contributes ; extending as they do towards Red Cliff Point. The fine cliff scenery extends past Osmington Mills, in headland after headland, until St. Aldhelm's Head is reached in the far distance.

To the southward, at the entrance to the Harbour, juts out the Nothe a high, grass-clad ridge, which belongs to the older portion of the town, and has guarded it from the days when it served to protect it from disputes with the " quarrel-some inhabitants of Portland."

Modern Weymouth is a pleasant holiday resort with little that is picturesque or old-world about it. Its most interesting features are to be found in the vicinity of the Quay, and the more historical portion across the harbour. The inner portion of the harbour, behind the town, is connected with the older part by a bridge. From this one obtains a good view of the quay, the ships, the waterside types, and the older warehouses of faded red brick, dating from the days when Weymouth had considerable trade and commerce. This is the part of the town beloved by artists ; where there are narrow lanes, and still some few houses with bow windows of small diamond panes, and with lodging houses frequented by pilots and seamen ashore.

Many of the little shops in this quarter have a charm and pictuesqueness that has survived from the times of King George's visit to the town for the sea bathing, and the gay doings recorded in *The Trumpet Major*.

Weymouth has had its history, however. It was " several times attacked by French pirates," probably privateers ; who raided it and burned many of the houses, and more than once captured a vessel or two in the harbour, and carried them off to French ports, notwithstanding the stout resistance made by the inhabitants.

Indeed, Weymouth, like many Wessex coastal towns, has had a chequered and even important history. Its first charter was given it by King Ethelred about A.D. 978, but somewhat strangely this is found preserved in the archives of Winchester Cathedral !

A little less than seventy-five years later Weymouth and Melcombe passed into the possesion of the Abbey of Cerne Abbas as part and parcel of the Manor of Radipole. But in 1280 Melcombe was converted into a Royal demesne, and became known as Melcombe Regis. It formed part of the dowry of Eleanor of Castile, Queen Consort of Edward I. By the middle of the fourteenth century the town had attained to a position of considerable importance, and was able to supply no less than twenty ships and two hundred and sixty-four men for the siege of Calais. As a result it was in the ensuing years subject to reprisals and attacks by the French.

By the reign of Elizabeth, Weymouth had much increased in size and importance ; and when summoned to assist in repelling the Armada, sent " six ships of good tonnage," named *Golden Lion*, 120 tons ; *Galleon*, 100 tons ; *Sutton*, 70 tons ; *Expedition*, 70 tons ; *Heath Hen*, 60 tons ; and *Catherine*, 60 tons ; " all of which were a great aid to Sir Francis Drake."

A Dennis Bond of Weymouth was summoned by a special letter from Oliver Cromwell to attend Parliament for the two boroughs of Melcombe Regis and Weymouth. The letter addressed in the Protector's own hand ran " Haste, Post Haste. For the special service of the Commonwealth. For Dennis Bond, Esq. . . . These. O. Cromwell." In return for the honour the Protector had shown him " the said Dennis Bond during the Session of 1654 moved that the Crown and title of King should be offered to the Protector."

During the Civil War the two boroughs had undoubtedly been for the King, and both Roundhead and Royalist armies contended hotly for their possession. And till comparatively quite recent times houses and buildings in the vicinity of the Harbour were still standing that bore traces of bombardment, and here and there cannon ball and bullet holes were to be seen.

Weymouth has had a number of notable sons, who represented it in Parliament. Among them may be mentioned Sir William Penn, the father of the founder of Pennsylvania, who was born at Weymouth in 1620, entered the navy at the age of fourteen, and became Vice-Admiral of England during the first war with the Dutch. Sir Christopher Wren, architect of St. Paul's Cathedral, also sat for the

Borough ; as did the famous artist Sir James Thornhill, one of whose pictures, representing " The Last Supper," forms the altar piece in St. Mary's Church, Melcombe Regis.

The rise of Weymouth, as a watering place and seaside resort dates from the time so vividly described by Hardy in his novel, to which reference has previously been made. The discovery of its possibilities as a social resort must be credited to H.R.H. the Duke of Gloucester, who visited Weymouth and became so pleased with it that, about 1780, he built himself a house on the Esplanade, known as Gloucester Lodge, which ultimately became the Gloucester Hotel. The mere fact of this royal patronage had the effect of leading the townsfolk and public authorities to take steps to improve its, then scanty, social amenities. Assembly Rooms, Pump Rooms, coffee taverns, billiards rooms and dance halls came speedily into being. And " Baths," in imitation of the establishment at Bath, were, on a more modest scale, instituted ; in one of the main streets. But Weymouth had been awakened from some of its lethargy some quarter of a century before the arrival of the Duke of Gloucester.

A Bath doctor had a rich patient named Ralph Allen, who became seriously ill, and consulted his medical man, whose name has not come down to us. The Doctor is said to have taken the remarkably daring step or recommending the then almost unheard of cure of bathing in the open sea. The patient decided to try the treatment, and came to Weymouth.

A machine was constructed so that the invalid could enter the water with some degree of decorum and privacy. And doubtless this contraption was the father of the succeeding less cumbersome ' bathing machine ' of Victorian Days, and the grandfather, or perhaps one should say, the great-grand-father of the succeeding tents and huts used by modern bathers. Not long after Ralph Allen's daring attempt to regain his health, by such, as were considered, drastic means, a writer reported the rapid growth of the town's popularity, " from the vast concourse of polite company by which it has become now frequented for sea bathing."

It was, however, in 1789 that the sign manual of patronage was set upon the town by the coming of George III, Queen Charlotte, and three of the young Princesses; who, leaving Windsor Castle early in the morning of June 24th, 1789 in three carriages, after breaking the journey for a few days in the New Forest, arrived at Weymouth.

Hardy, of course, gives in *The Trumpet Major*, a graphic and arresting picture of the Royal activities while at Weymouth. Especially of the great review, held on the downs, of the forces gathered to resist the feared invasion by Napoleon. A picture of turmoil and pageantry that can scarcely be equalled.

And on the downs above Osmington there is the famous " White Horse," carved in the turf of the chalk hill. A huge equestrian figure with a cocked hat; intended to represent King George himself!

Not far away, and much visited, hidden in the picturesque downs, is Sutton Poyntz, the " Overcombe " of *The Trumpet Major* and the chief scene of that spirited novel. And hard-by is the Mill where Miller Loveday, Ann Garland and her mother lived. But the mill described by Hardy is in reality at Upwey, some four miles north of Weymouth, where there is a noted " Wishing Well" which, in summer is beautiful with its surrounding trees and many ferns. The legend can be guessed by the name, which is that anyone drinking the water, and at the same time having a wish, will have it granted. But they must throw some of the water over the left shoulder while wishing!

To return to Weymouth again. Not only Hardy, but another novelist, of a generation before his time, has put on record the ' doings ' of the King and members of his family and *entourage*. For Miss Fanny Burney, the authoress, of *Evelina* and *Cecilia* afterwards wrote of the Royal visit of eleven weeks duration which was followed by others for some years. She tells us " The preparations of festive loyalty were universal. Not a child could be met that had not a bandeau round its head, cap or hat, of " God Save the King." All the bargemen wore cockades ; and even the bathing women had it in large coarse girdles round their waists."

And we are told, by another writer, that the inhabitants of the town, and those who had flocked to it " dogged the footsteps of Royalty all day long, calling out " God Save the King," and pressing their noses against the window panes when the Royal party were dining in Gloucester House."

The first time the King bathed, Miss Burney who was at Court, and attendant on the Queen as a Mistress of the Robes, tells us " he was surprised, as well he might be, when he had popped his head under water, that a band of music, concealed in a neighbouring machine, started playing " God Save great George our King."

Naturally many stories collected around the Royal visitors, who, at least so far as King George was concerned, appear to have moved amongst the people at times very informally. On the occasion of the presentation of an address of welcome to the King there is a good story recorded.

When the Mayor advanced to make the presentation— instead of kneeling as he was expected to do, he took the Queen's hand to shake it. A Colonel Gwynn, who was acting as master of the ceremonies, curtly told the Mayor he should have kneeled.

His reply was " Sir, I cannot,"

" Everyone has to do so, sir," the Colonel exclaimed.

Then the Mayor blushed deeply, and said, with evident embarrassment, " Damme— sir, I have a wooden leg ! "

Another story, at the time well-authenticated, runs as follows. The King was out riding in the countryside not far from Upwey. And he passed a field in which, although it was harvest time, only one woman was at work. The King was known to be of an enquiring disposition, and he stopped, and asked the woman where all her companions had gone. She replied, without knowing who was speaking to her :

" They have gone to town to see the King."

" And why did not you go as well ? "

" Oh ! " came the reply, " I wouldn't give as much as a pin to see 'un "—adding " Besides, the fools that are down to town to see 'un will lose a day's work by it, which is more than I can afford to do, for I have five children to work for."

The King is said to have put his hand, as Kings generally are said to do on such occasions, into his pocket, and to have given the woman some money. Remarking : " Well, you can tell your companions, who are gone to see the King, that the King came to see you."

In those days the seafront at Weymouth must have presented a gay and interesting spectacle, as we are told the countryfolk for miles around were accustomed to flock into the town to see the Georgian dandies with their ' clouded ' canes, strutting along the Esplanade, jewelled snuff boxes in hand. And chairmen bearing stately ladies, rouged, patched and crinolined, attended, many of them, by courtiers in the gay-coloured attire of that time.

And a writer of the period, a sort of ' special correspondent ' of a London ' news-letter,' told how " many folk come into the town daily to see His Majesty and the Court bathing in the sea water half-a-furlong out from the shore. And sometimes the crowd would be so great on the sands that people are pushed into the sea against their will."

Regarding the conduct of card parties, balls and ' routs ' there were curious rules drawn up. For example, lest " ruffling " or disputes should by any chance arise, gentlemen were compelled to leave their swords at the door. And on Tuesdays and Fridays they were not allowed to appear in boots at dances ! Presumably riding boots.

Portland, called by Hardy " the Isle of Slingers " in *The Well Beloved*, is not, of course, an island but a peninsula.

Seen from the White Nose, or Lulworth one realises the aptness and accuracy of Hardy's description of it, " the isle . . . . lying on the sea to the south-west of these, like a great crouching animal tethered to the mainland." That, is, indeed, how the distant view of Portland across the bay, has always struck me, since I first read the novel.

Portland is so unique a part of Wessex that it is well worth visiting. One can easily live the pages of the novel as one ascends the principal street, " the street of Wells " leading steeply up to Fortune's Well, the island's chief town, with its severe-looking stone houses and its equally plain Church. At the top of the climbing street one is on the ' roof ' of the island, and has come to a region of stone quarries ; and, on the west side of the road, are narrow by-ways which disappear from sight as though they had dropped over the edge of the cliff.

The prospect that meets the eye is bare and apparently somewhat cumbered with fragments of masonry strewn about ; and where one might hope for herbage there is rubble ; and in place of gardens, except here and there, are heaps of quarry chippings. But there are a few picturesque old cottages, belonging, at least in some cases, to the last half of the seventeenth century, and the best of them have stone, mullioned windows with tiny panes, and some, porches and picturesque gables. And, in Hardy's time some were thatched. The Prison used to be the great attraction for visitors, who spent their time watching the convicts at work.

But Portland has at least one beauty spot in the little Cove strangely named Church Hope. It lies on the eastern side, a narrow little glen running down to the sea and a small beach. And on the cliff above it stands the chief Portland dwelling and ' object of interest,' Pennsylvania Castle. A rather foursquare castellated type of building, erected in 1800 for John Penn, the grandson of the founder of Pennsylvania. John Penn was at the time Governor of the island.

It is just here that one has a surprise in that there is a lovely garden, and on the adjacent cliffs some wild flowers are to be seen in due season. Round the cove below are fishermen's huts, and the ruins of the old Parish Church of Portland, destroyed by a landslip which only left ivy-covered walls and an air of sad neglect.

One recalls the fact that many of the scenes in Hardy's novel *The Well Beloved* are set in Portland; at Hope-Cove and its Church, Pennsylvania Castle, and Sandsfoot Castle, or Henry VIII's Castle. The last mentioned, standing on a grass-clad spur overlooking the Harbour, was built in the year 1539, when the country was in fear of invasion. In Leland's time it was referred to as "a right goodly and warlyke castle," but now is a fragmentary ruin. Another, on the eastern side of the island, and almost in its centre is Bow and Arrow, or Rufus's Castle, of which little more than the Keep remains standing.

The two lighthouses, both at the southern end of the island seldom fail to attract visitors, and from nearby one obtains the sight of a magnificent stretch of coast scenery east and west, as well as unrivalled views of the Channel. The lower lighthouse was built in 1789; and the higher in 1817 and rebuilt half-a-century later. They both contain extremely powerful lights, and at specified times may be visited. A noted smugglers' cave, known as Cave's Hole of enormous size, lies near the lower lighthouse, into which in stormy weather the seas break with terrific force. Quite close is the famous Portland Bill, and there also is the Pulpit Rock; and, off shore, the Race. In the whirlpool waters of which, from the time of the Danish invaders, many a vessel has been lost.

Distant from Weymouth by road about 10 miles, and also reached by rail from Broadway junction, is Abbotsbury, at the back of the famous Chesil Beach; picturesquely situated in a valley at the western end of the Fleet. The latter is a lagoon or stretch of water some six miles in length and of varying width starting from Wyke Regis, just outside Weymouth.

Abbotsbury is the seat of the Earl of Ilchester, and is a place of great antiquity mentioned in *The Trumpet Major* as Abbotsea Beach. It appears to have been known by the name long before the Monastery was founded in the reign of Canute, probably in the year 1017, by Orc, the King's Seneschel. There used to be a prosperous mackerel fishery in connection with Abbotsbury, and for the right of fishing an annual payment is made by each boat to the Earl of Ilchester. The lord of the manor is, too, by ancient custom, entitled to the best, or first fish of each kind taken by each boat, paying a fixed nominal sum for it which was fixed by the Abbot as follows : 6d. for a salmon ; 4d. for a turbot ; and other fish in proportion.

One fears that Abbotsbury is usually somewhat over-looked by tourists and holiday makers in Wessex ; but the village is well worth seeing, and has several unique features. It is a pretty place, neat and clean ; with some charming cottages and houses, some of which date back to the 16th century. They are stone built, and many are thatched ; or have stone slab roofs. Much of the material for building them was obviously derived from the Abbey, when the foundation was suppressed, and ultimately became derelict.

One, as a consequence, finds stone-mullioned windows to some of the houses ; and others with fragments of ecclesiastical architecture incorporated in their walls, and even the section of a Gothic arch ! Some of the buildings were evidently the domestic offices of the Abbey, which were adapted as dwellings and farmhouses. The ancient manor house, of many gables, its porch, with a room over it, and a fine stone staircase leading to the entrance never fail to charm the visitor.

The Abbey was of great size and magnificence, and, at its dissolution was given to Sir Giles Strangways, in whose family it still remains. During the Civil War the place suffered severely, as the Abbey house and even the Church had been garrisoned for King Charles by the then owner Colonel Strangways. In 1644 the village was attacked by the Parliamentary forces under Sir Anthony Ashley Cooper, and, after severe fighting, was captured and the house was burnt down. A contemporary account gives the following details : " Our soldiers, (the Parliamentarians) were forced to wrench open the windows with iron bars, pouring in faggots of furze fired, set the whole house in a flaming fire, so that it was not possible to be quenched . . . . " quarter was at first denied to, the occupants. But, later, we are told " Colonel and Major Sidenham riding to the other side of the house gave them quarter, upon which our men fell into the house to plunder, and could not be by any of their commanders drawn out, though they were told the enemy's magazine was near the fire, and if they stayed would prove their ruin, which accordingly fell out, for the powder, taking fire, blew up all that were in the house."

Of the Abbey nothing now remains save an ivy-clad wall.

The Parish Church of St. Nicholas, though attacked and captured, was little harmed externally, and is a fine building with an impressive square embattled tower. All around are fragments of the ancient Abbey. Among the remains are a number of stone coffins, about which the villagers used to tell wierd tales. In the church porch there is an ancient coffin lid on which is carved a figure supposed to be that of an abbot, holding a book and carrying a staff ; and over the west door is a curious figure said to represent the Trinity. The interior of the church consists of a nave, and aisles, separated by pillars carrying pointed arches. There is a beautifully carved pulpit ; pierced in two places with bullet holes, which are said to have been fired during the attack on the church by the Parliamentary forces.

Douglas Snowdon

The Barn
Abbotsbury   "Abbotsea"

A strangely beautiful thing, that should not be missed, is a woman's head in ancient stained glass in one of the windows. It is supposed to be that of St. Catherine. The colours have faded, but the expression of the face is unforgettable. Her hands are clasped, and her head has a yellow halo, and a wimple encircles her face.

Abbotsbury Castle, the seat of the Earl of Ilchester stands on rising ground about a mile from the village. It is in the Gothic style of architecture, and commands a wide view of the West Bay and the Fleet. Its fine and extensive gardens are famous, containing as they do beautiful flowers of all kinds and many semi-tropical plants and trees.

The famous Swannery and Decoy for wildfowl, for which Abbotsbury is widely known, date right back to the middle ages, and a mention is made of them in the reign of Elizabeth, the lands being " held by John Strangeways Esquire, of the Queen in chief." The Swannery is situated on the margin of West Fleet and is enclosed by a high wall. It is several acres in extent, which are covered with palms, willows, shrubs, and water weeds, on the last named of which the wild fowl feed, and amid which the swans build their nests. The latter number normally between 1,000 and 1,200, according to the season of the year. It is a sight well worth seeing, and visitors are admitted on certain days of the week.

Another attraction at Abbotsbury is the famous St. Catherin's Chapel, standing high on a hill about half-a-mile south-west of the village. It is supposed to have been built as an expiatory chapel in the reign of Edward IV, about 1470. But it is thought probable it has a much earlier origin. There is a four storied octagonal tower at the north-west angle. The length of the building is 45 ft. and width 15 ft. The roof is finely arched ; and some of the ornaments still remain.

The Monastery tithe-barn is said to the largest in the south-west of England, and is a fine remnant of the Monastic buildings. It is approached by a large gate-house, in which, tradition asserts, the last of the Abbots was confined and starved to death. The barn, of which the greater portion is still standing, must have originally been at least 300 feet in length, and remains a well-preserved and interesting example of mediæval architecture.

One of the most remarkable features in Wessex is the famous Chesil Bank or Beach, which, starting at Deadman's Bay on the western side of Portland where it joins the mainland, extends along the West Bay for a distance of almost fifteen miles in the direction of Bridport. It is an immense bank or ridge of pebbles ; varying in width from 200 yards at Portland, with a height of 42 ft. above high-water mark, to 170 yards in width and a height of 23 ft. at Abbotsbury. The word *chesil* is Anglo-Saxon for pebble. The stones vary very much in size being largest at the Portland end, where they are some of them almost the size of a child's head or small coconut, and are very small pebbles where the beach meets the Bridport cliffs. So regular, however, is the decrease in size, that fishermen, and in the old days smugglers, coming ashore even in the dark could easily guess their actual whereabouts by the size of the stones.

Upon Chesil Bank there have been many wrecks, from the days of the Roman invasion of Britain, down to modern times, and rescue is rendered very difficult owing to the immense rollers and ' undertow ' when a gale is raging in West Bay. Deadman's Bay is, truly, a death trap, and a little more than a century and a quarter ago, a fleet of transports was wrecked there with the loss of more than 1,000 lives. In the year 1748 a treasure ship with £50,000 aboard, in gold, named *The Hope of Amsterdam* went ashore, and became a complete wreck on the Bank.

There are many stories relating to the wreckers, and smugglers among the number ; but never before nor since, have such scenes of horror " riot, violence and barbarity " been seen there, as on that occasion. We are told by a contemporary writer that " for ten days the ravening mob held the beach in defiance of all authority. Fighting and struggling for the gold coins washed ashore ; drunk with the spirits from the kegs that had also washed up."

CHAPTER V

A GROUP OF INTERESTING AND HISTORIC CENTRAL AND NORTHERN TOWNS

ILGRIMS IN WESSEX will find in its central and northern portion a group of towns, which figure not only more or less prominently as the places in which Hardy has placed the scene of several of his novels and short stories, but are historically and in other ways interesting.

Sherborne, which Hardy calls Sherton Abbas is one of these. It figures largely in *The Woodlanders* ; in two short stories in his volume *A Group of Noble Dames, Squire Patrick's Lady*, and *Anna, Lady Baxby* ; also in one scene in *Tess of the D'Urbervilles*. The town lies close to the borders of Somerset, pleasantly and picturesquely situated on the southern slope of a steep hill overlooking the valley of the Yeo.

One easily reaches it from almost any part of Wessex, by rail, or by excellent and usually picturesque roads.

Although Sherborne is more old-fashioned, than actually beautiful, it has much of interest still clinging to it. And possesses a magnificent Abbey Church, and a famous and ancient Grammar School.

Also remaining are some interesting old houses, and beautiful walks on the south side of the river ; which, from its clarity, in Anglo-Saxon times originated its name Scirburne. The " Scir " meaning bright, and " burne " brook, the Yeo or Ivel.

Though the ancient records of the town are somewhat meagre, there is little doubt that even in the eighth century it was a place of considerable importance. For King Ina, about

A.D. 707, is said to have founded a magnificent, and what afterwards became a very rich, Abbey of great repute ; and, as early as A.D. 705 the town was chosen as the seat of a bishopric. According to William of Malmesbury the civilising influence of the monastic institution was sadly needed, for he tells us that the people of the vicinity were but half-civilised barbarians. " Wherefore the Holy man Aldhelm," the first of the line of twenty-seven bishops " used to place himself upon the bridge near the town and stop the passers by singing ballads of his own composing. By this means he gradually gained the favour and attention of the populace ; and, by mixing grave and religious things with those of a jocular kind, insensibly by this means succeeded in turning their attention towards religion better than he could have done by mere sermonising."

The old bishops of Sherborne appear to have been of a very militant type, for several fell in battle with the Danes. One of these was Asser, the friend and biographer of Alfred the Great. The last of the Bishops of Sherborne was Herman, when the See, in 1078 was removed to Old Sarum.

At one period the town became the capital of Wessex, and was also at that time in size the second city of England after Winchester.

Its situation in the far corner of Dorset and on high ground made it easy of defence ; and here the English held their own against the raiding Northmen. And here were buried Ealhstan, who was the first to oppose the Danes successfully, and two brothers of King Alfred, King Ethelbald and King Ethelbert.

At the end of the tenth century Ethelred the Unready gave permission for Bishop Wulfsey III, to make Sherborne Monastery one of the Benedictine Order. We are told that at about that time the Second Advent was engaging the thought of the people ; and that " very severe reforms in the interest of religion and morality were brought about."

One of the most noticeable things in connection with the beautiful Abbey is that its gradual growth can be traced in its

Sherborne
"Sherton Abbas"

architecture, which reflects the different periods of the religious life and influence upon the community. In 1436 a quarrel arose between the monks and the townspeople, regarding which of two fonts, the old or a new one, should be used when the children of the town were baptized. The monks blocked a certain door, used by the townspeople, to prevent them entering a part of the Church, and they, greatly incensed, revenged themselves by an unseemly pealing of bells, which disturbed the monastic services.

The Bishop of Salisbury was appealed to for a decision, and he very wisely declared that the ancient font should be used for all purposes, and the new one removed. But this did not appease the townsfolk, there was a riot ; and during the disturbance " a priest shot an arrow with fire to it, into part of the abbey, which lodged in the roof, which in the part where the arrow struck was thatched, set it on fire and much damage was done to the church and the lead and bells were melted."

After this catastrophe the eastern wing was pulled down, and the present beautiful choir erected, during the time of Abbot Bradford (1437-59). The old nave was then rebuilt in the Perpendicular style. The transcepts still retain their Norman masonry, but they have large Perpendicular windows. The three tower arches, with their plain Norman semi-circles are out of character with the richness of their surroundings.

The great tenor bell of the Abbey was the gift of Cardinal Wolsey, and was brought over by him from Tournai, of which he was bishop. The bell bears the following inscription :—

By Wolesy's gift I mesure time for all :
To mirth, to grief, to church, I serve to call.

One cannot fail to admire the great beauty of the interior of the church, and especially noticeable is the roof of the south transept, which is of black Irish oak.

The details of this fine and interesting building are well worth careful study by architects and lovers of beauty. The glass in the clerestory windows contains figures of the Saints and Bishops of Sherborne, and the reredos, depicts in high relief, the Ascension and The Last Supper, and has a moulding of Caen stone. Also noticeable and exquisite are the throne, sedilia, and the carved work of the stalls.

Of the original Abbey buildings, the remains, once considerable, on the north side of the church have been incorporated in the buildings of the well-known Grammar School. The present dining-hall dates from 1670, and was the old school room. In it is a statue of Edward VI, who refounded the school in 1550. The statue dates from 1614. It cost the sum of £9 5s. 4d. and is the work of one Godfrey Arnold. And in the school accounts are various entries of 6d. " For washing the King."

The school buildings are both interesting and very picturesque, and consist of rambling halls and buildings of many periods scattered about the Abbey grounds, and are always affording the wandering visitor surprises of delightful courtyards, pleasant lawns and half subterranean cloisters. Many buildings being creeper-clad blending effectively with the yellow stone.

Among the notable fragments of the Monastery are the Abbot's Hall, standing on an undercroft of Late-Norman work. with a 15th century timber roof. The building is now used as the school Chapel. Other most interesting buildings are the kitchen, and the Guesten Hall. The latter now the fine Library of the School, which contains upwards of 7,000 volumes. Among them are several rarities, including copies of " Matthew Paris," printed in London in 1571 ; and an Aldine " Euripides," printed in Venice in 1503.

The boys who obtain studies in a quaint and beautiful house dating from the same period, which has a fine canopied doorway, are indeed fortunate. Once it was the Abbot's Lodging.

The Headmaster's garden is usually in Spring, Summer and Autumn a blaze of colour. The soil must be good, and probably the garden being on the site of the old fishponds of the monks is also beneficial.

The Lady Chapel stands to the left of a quiet square ; a 13th century building, now a master's house, with Tudor windows. A more delightful and picturesque home could not easily be imagined.

A seat of learning for 1,200 years ever since St. Adhelm's time, when he founded a school here, it has still remained one with a high and enviable reputation.

There are many other quaint, beautiful and interesting things to see in this quiet and charming town, and among these the Almshouse, with its Chapel and delightful cloisters, originally called the Hospital of St. John Baptist, should not be missed by anyone for whom beautiful architecture has an alluring charm. Erected in 1448, founded on the lines of an older organisation of 1406, it is a veritable gem of its kind.

Nor should what remains of Sherborne Castle, the fragments of which, ivy-clad and age-old, stand on a small wooded hill, be overlooked. Once it was a stronghold of importance, and the residence of the Bishops in the days of William the Conqueror. In the reign of Edward VI, it was given to the Protector Somerset, and finally passed into the possession of Sir Walter Raleigh, who, before he fell out of favour, made it over to his son. But, owing to an error in the deed, made by the copying clerk, King James I was able to seize the property.

Tradition states there was a strange mediæval curse placed upon the Castle and its surrounding lands by a knight named Osmund, who was made Earl of Dorset by William the Conqueror, with a grant of the Castle and barony. After a while the Earl entered a religious life, and became in time Bishop of Sarum. He gave Sherborne and other lands to the bishopric. His curse was, we are told, as follows : " That whosoever should take those lands from the bishopric, or diminish in great or small, should be accursed, not only in this world, but also in the world to come, unless in his lifetime he made restitution thereof."

This curse seems to have prevailed in a number of instances. The Montacutes, the first to gain possession of the lands and Castle, after the Dissolution of the Monasteries by Henry VIII, became an extinct family; the next owner the Duke of Somerset, left the Castle for London, the Tower and execution; Sir Walter Raleigh lost the property, and then also went to the Tower and block; Prince Henry died very soon after he became possessed of the property; the next owner, Robert Carr, Earl of Somerset ended his life in shame and ignominy. It then reverted to the Crown and was given by King James I, when he acquired it from Sir Walter Raleigh, to Sir George Digby, afterwards created Earl of Bristol.

During the War between Charles I and his Parliament the Castle was very soon attacked by the Parliamentary forces under the command of the Earl of Bedford; and was defended by the Marquis of Hertford. It was not then captured, but three years later, when under the governorship of Sir Lewis Digby, it was attacked by General Fairfax, and capitulated after a siege of sixteen days. Shortly afterwards the Castle was destroyed by orders of the Parliament; and eventually some of the material was taken and used for the building of the present mansion of the Digby family, and the Church at Castleton.

The last historical event of any importance connected with Sherborne was when William of Orange landed in 1688 at Brixham, Torbay, to become an English King, with Mary, as Queen, daughter of James II, who had fled his realm. William paused on his way to London at Sherborne, and slept at the present mansion of the Digby family.

Sherborne of today is one of the most picturesquely placed towns in Hardy's Wessex, and even now its life is marked by just that impression of old-time peace and absence of ' drive ' and turmoil, that one often finds in other Wessex towns.

Shaftesbury, Hardy's Shaston, is just such another ancient and historic town which seems to have been able, to have kept itself very much aloof " from the fret and fume that men to-day call progress," as one writer has put it. From Sherborne to reach Shaftesbury, some sixteen miles distant, one passes through some of the most pleasing scenery and countryside to be found in Wessex, and crosses the famous and lovely Blackmore Vale about midway between the two places.

In this fertile and charming valley, through which the Cale with devious windings flows to meet the Stour ; one has luxuriant pastures and a district still comparatively unknown to strangers, although the rise and popularity of hiking and of motor touring of late years has somewhat more familiarised it to holiday makers. Formerly it was known as the White Hart Forest, which in by-gone days was one of Henry III's Royal hunting grounds. There is a legend that the King levied a perpetual fine upon the inhabitants of the forest region because a gentleman when hunting killed a white hart, which the King had several times spared because of its beauty.

Here, too are to be seen oaks such as have made the Hampshire New Forest famous for centuries. The prospect from the heights above the Vale is a most beautiful one, the fields are rich in pasturage, and present a contrast to the barer downs southward near the coast. It was at Rushay Farm near the southern end of the long valley, that William Barnes, was born, and he was a great admirer of the beauties of Blackmoor Vale. He called it, and there is no better description " the valley of sunny slopes, shady lanes, woody dales, picturesque trees and rivulets " and adds, " You cannot proceed a quarter of a mile without seeing a pretty cottage with its honeysuckled porch, and healthy children playing about."

It is through such scenery as this that one approaches Shaftesbury, the Shaston of *Tess of the D'Urbervilles*, along the main road to the town. It is truly a hill town, built on a steep-sided solitary chalk ridge, with but a single easy road to it, and as one climbs up to it it has a marvellously picturesque appearance, and on a fine summer day in the early morning it seems to possess a strangely individual atmosphere of its own, compounded of sunshine and mist, with blue smoke driving across its roofs. The houses built on the side of the hill or on the hillcrest, and amid the trees that shade its southern slopes, have almost a Continental look.

Shaftesbury is what they call in Wessex " an old ancient town." Indeed some authorities are inclined to believe it was there before the Romans climbed up its steep hill, and that the present town was founded by Alfred the Great in or about A.D. 880 ; or, say, more than one thousand years ago. It is quite possible that this is so, for then it offered so strong a strategic position, with its sharply projecting natural rampart, and its environing country of dense forest and swamps, and the additional great advantage of offering a good lookout in several directions.

Shaftesbury has had several names. Its first one was Caer Pallador, and by the time the Domesday Book was compiled for William the Conqueror in 1080 it was known as Sceptesberie. Next it fancied the name of Sophonia, and last became Shaston, which the countryfolk call it to this day, and unwittingly provided Hardy with one of those appropriate but thinly disguised names to which he was so partial.

In those early days one great disadvantage the town undoubtedly had. It was shortage of water. And more recently we are told that after the water carriers had toilsomely ascended the steep road they received a payment that today seems niggardly ; twopence for a horse load, and a farthing for a pail " if fetched upon the head."

Early in its history an Abbey was built, founded by Alfred the Great. It was a glorious building, and the head of the foundation, the Abbess of Shaftesbury, was Elgiva, the King's daughter, who was wealthy in gold and lands, and gave wonderful plate to the Abbey, and was buried here. Here it was that Edward the Martyr was ultimately buried ; brought from the little Saxon Church of St. Martin at Wareham.

The possession of the martyred saint's body at Shaftesbury led to it becoming a place of pilgrimage ; and, we are told, so marvellous were some of the cures brought about at the martyr's tomb that " the sick, sad and those seeking forgiveness of their sins flocked from all parts to the Abbey. In the Abbey also lay buried the Queen of Edmund Ironside, known as " the last hero of the old Royal line."

The nunnery was also founded by King Alfred, who, we are told, gave land to the church at Shaftesbury " to honour of God and the holy Virgin and for the health of his own soul."

The convent flourished until the middle of the sixteenth century and then the end came with the Dissolution of the Religious Houses. Shaftesbury, at the height of its ecclesiastical fame and magnificence, possessed no fewer than twelve churches, and of these but two, Holy Trinity and St. Peter's remain.

Unfortunately the former, the principal Church in the town, and once one of importance was pulled down, and entirely rebuilt in 1842, in a rather commonplace type of architecture, and consequently has little of interest or distinction.

St. Peter's is the solitary survial of Shaftesbury's great Ecclesiastical era. It is a 15th century building of the late Perpendicular period. The nave and north aisle are of the same length, and there is no chancel arch. But the western tower, which contains six bells is imposing, and the northern wall, in the High Street, is worth noting as it has a remarkably handsome battlemented parapet, and is ornamented with carved roses, pomegranates and portcullises, a form of decoration much favoured by artists and sculptors in the early part of the reign of Henry VIII.

On the North and South walls of the Belfry are inscriptions. Two lines of the rhymed verse on the South wall paint a picture of what the bell-ringers of the 16th century had to do :—

> Then in your ringing make no demur,
> But off your hat, your belts and spurs.

And there is an element of preachment in the lines found on the North wall :—

> What musick is there that compar'd may be
> To well-tun'd bells' enchanting melody ;
> Breaking with their sweet sound the willing air,
> And in the list'ning ear the soul ensnare.
> When bells ring round, and in their order be,
> They do denote how neighbours should agree.

On the bells themselves are some quaint inscriptions, the earliest of which dates from 1670. Two of the inscriptions are as follows :—

> While we join in cheerful sound,
> May love and loyalty abound.
> > H. Oram, C. warden
> > D. Wells, Aldbourne, fecit, 1776.

> When you hear me for to toll,
> Then pray God to save the soul.
> > Anno Domini 1672.   T.H.R.W.C.T.P.

Shaftesbury, when the struggle between King Charles I, and the Parliament arose, and ultimately led to the Civil War, was attacked, and changed hands several times. Also minor engagements were fought in its vicinity. On August 1645 a body of the "Clubmen"—an organisation that had been formed with a view to protect the town from both parties—were engaged in a skirmish with Parliamentarian forces led by Fleetwood, who had come over from Sherborne with a body of fifty horsemen. He succeeded in arresting fifty of the Clubmen, and a little later the main body was defeated by Cromwell himself at Hambledon Hill, some ten miles away.

Somewhat strangely, Shaftesbury, though so ancient a town, was not incorporated until the reign of Elizabeth, and did not receive its charter until the succeeding reign of James I.

Just outside Shaftesbury at East Stower, Henry Fielding, the great novelist and author of *Tom Jones* and *Amelia*, lived with his mother, and afterwards with his first wife, Charlotte Cradock, a noted beauty of Salisbury, who figures in his novel *Amelia*, "as Sophia Western." Two, at least of the characters in his novels are said to have been local people. Parson Trulliber, who was a curate at Motcombe, named Oliver. And a Rev. William Young, the incumbent of West Stower, generally supposed to have been the prototype of Fielding's Parson Adams.

Shaftesbury leaves a pleasant impression on the minds of those who visit it, chiefly because it is age-old, placid in its life, and so finely situated that one can scarcely go down any of the steep by-ways, without having a vista of the distant and charming scene from between the houses which cling, one may say, almost precariously, on the crest and slopes of its commanding hill. As Hardy truly wrote in *Jude the Obscure*, when Jude and Sue were for a time living there, " The sunsets are mostly beautiful from here, owing to the rays crossing the mist of the vale."

Mainly the houses, many of which are really old, are of red brick or stone, are undistinguished in architecture. But there are others of differing heights and more pleasingly irregular architecture, with stone mullioned bow and bay windows, and with narrow lanes between, with lichen-stained walls of gardens, over which, in Spring, boughs of white and pink apple blossom stray, for a brief time to add a touch of delicate colour and loveliness to the scene. How old, and in some cases decrepit these houses appear, as though age had infected them with the disabilities of average human beings of four score.

Yes, the town conveys the impression of great age. And ecclesiastical nomenclature survives, from its hey-day of importance, in many of the tiny streets and by-ways. Ancient taverns and pilgrim Inns having given their names to streets, as Angel Lane, for example; where once stood a pilgrim's Inn that may have rivalled that at Glastonbury, founded by Abbot John de Selwood in 1475, now the George Inn, famous the world over. And Bell Street, where there was once an Inn of the name for the use of pilgrims. And Magdalen's Almshouse of unknown antiquity. It is Bymport, or Bind Port (or gate) of Edward IV's days that has also given its name to a picturesque street. In which the curious can find Phillotson's school mentioned in *Jude the Obscure*, and where, in a small house, Sue had stayed.

CHAPTER VI

SOME NORTHERN AND WESTERN WESSEX
TOWNS.

I T IS IN REACHING some of the smaller towns and villages in
north and west Wessex, through picturesque lanes, over
breezy uplands and often through a charming countryside that pleasure is experienced by the pilgrim in Wessex ;
rather than by reason of the size or importance of the places
themselves. But, as the backgrounds of Hardy's novels,
poems and tales, these have an added attraction, and even
importance.

Sturminster Newton, called by Hardy Stourcastle, where,
for two or three years after their marriage, he and his first wife
lived at " Riverside," to which he referred in his diary of 1876
as " a pretty cottage overlooking the Dorset Stour." They
left the house in the middle of March 1878 to make their
permanent home at " Max Gate," Dorchester.

In its early days Sturminster possessed a Minster, a Manor
house, and, according to Leland, ' a new town,' which has
served to give it its double-barrelled name. All of which
save the latter have vanished. It is mentioned also in the
Domesday Book, and appears in *Tess of the D'Urbervilles*.
The town is charmingly situated with the River Stour winding
round about it, and stretches of evergreen water-meadows
environing its outskirts. It is a place of great antiquity,
claiming connection with Alfred the Great ; and its Manor
was given by King Edgar to the monks at Glastonbury.
Behind the town rise the hills stretching from Hambledon
to Bulbarrow.

Coming from the south one approaches the town across an old stone bridge having six pointed arches, connecting Sturminster with Newton, and at the latter there are, on a mound, traces of an ancient castle. Looking along an avenue of trees there appears an irregular line of houses on both sides of the road. Some with gardens, and of various types of architecture, and some are above the level of the road.

There is, however, a definite centre to the town, its ' Square ' to which all roads lead. There are two picturesque old inns, one with a thatched roof with dormer windows in it, and there is an opening leading to the stable yard, with a small room over the passage, all recalling old coaching days. Close to the Church is the school where William Barnes was educated ; very much, from its appearance, one may guess, as when he was a pupil. The old mill is picturesque and worth seeing, as it is well preserved, and is one still left of its type to be seen in Wessex.

Few who come to Sturminster Newton, we fancy, but will wish to go the five miles or so northward to Marnhull. The Marlott of Hardy's novels, and the birthplace and home in her early life of *Tess of the D'Urbervilles*. One can do so by pleasant roads, though the village itself is, it is true, somewhat disappointing. It stands on rising ground above the River Stour and has a long straggling street, and appears today in no way to justify Leland's flattering description of " a good uplandishe towne." However, like so many other towns in Wessex of its present size, it may have been of importance in the past.

Once there was an annual bull-baiting held in the Valley Meadow, as the scene of the event is called ; which took place on the third of May. The sport in those days was popluar enough ; but on several occasions led " to riot and fightings, with harm to those who were onlookers." The contending bulls, we are told came from neighbouring villages, whose inhabitants accompanied the animals, and the fighting and

Marnhull
(the "Crown")

House Shotover

Marlott

disputes, that often took place, arose as to the relative merits of the contending bulls. The sport was put a stop to in 1763 ; much to the disgust of the inhabitants.

Marnhull's great possession is its particularly fine church, the tower of which provides a striking landmark for the countryfolk many miles around. There are several memorials of note in the church. Among them, on one of the tombs, the recumbent figure of a knight in armour, said to be that of Thomas Howard, Viscount Bindon, who died in 1582. On either side of him are his two wives. The alabaster effigies are much mutilated, which is said to have come about " by reason of so much of the alabaster has been stole to make dies for coining." The knight is shown as a very tall and robust man ; the wives are small, and charming in the old-time costumes they are shown wearing, even including necklaces, which, as are the garments, identical in every particular.

Collectors of epitaphs will find a rich store in church and churchyard. One, written by a rector for his clerk, who died at the great age of 94 in 1752, runs as follows :—

> " Here under this stone
>   Lie Ruth and old John,
>   Who smoked all his life
>   And so did his wife ;
>   And now there's no doubt
>   But their pipes are put out.
>   Be it said without joke
>   That life is but smoke ;
>   Though you live to fourscore,
>   'Tis a whiff and no more."

Which proves that smoking by women is not a modern innovation.

From Tess's home village, and the old "Crown Inn" Hardy had in mind and called the "Pure Drop," which was destined to ruin her father, John Durbeyfield, and, in the end, his family, we turn south-westward to Cerne Abbas, called by Hardy Abbot's Cernel, a little town of much picturesqueness and historic interest, reached along pleasant roads and some delightful scenery.

It lies tucked away in a gap in the chalk hills by which it is environed ; almost midway between Dorchester and Sherborne and due north of the former. Once, as is the case with many Wessex towns it was a dignified and even important place, largely on account of its fine Abbey, founded by Aethelmar, Earl of Devon and Cornwall, about A.D. 987.

The Abbey went through the usual vicissitudes of those times of Danish marauders, and was on several occasions plundered. But " for the sake of their souls never permitted by the pious to suffer in the long run." As years passed the Abbey grew rich and magnificent, and out of the original settlement at Cerne a town grew up, which the Abbey for a time sheltered and in some measure fostered.

It played its part in the tempestuous and devastating Wars of the Roses. To it, after the battle of Barnet, in which Warwick the King maker, who had espoused the Lancastrian cause, was killed, and the cause lost, came in 1471 Queen Margaret and her son, for whom she had fought so pertinaciously to secure him the Lancastrian succession to the throne.

She had landed at Weymouth the very day that Warwick had been defeated and slain ; lured back to England from France, by the fact that so powerful a noble had espoused her cause. They came to Cerne across the hills, and sought sanctuary in the Abbey. She did not, however, rest there long under defeat, for she put herself at the head of the Beauforts, and marched towards Wales, encountering and being defeated by the Yorkists on reaching Tewkesbury. She and her son were taken prisoners. And that was the end of the Lancastrian cause. Margaret was allowed to return again to France ; after her son had been foully murdered in cold blood.

The first Abbot of Cerne, was a scholar. He translated his "Homilies," written in Latin, into Anglo-Saxon, which provided "written in very easy Anglo-Saxon, the best book for the student beginning a study of that language," according to Mr. Wright, who is an accepted authority.

The remains of the beautiful Abbey are but slight. The fine Gatehouse, however, is in a fair state of preservation. It stands environed by trees, and with its most delightful two-storied oriel window, above the groined entrance, where the shields of the founder and of the foundation itself, are still traceable.

Of the Abbey House, once the home of Denzil Holles, the brother-in-law of Strafford, little remains. The fine and ancient tithe barn is now part of a farmhouse ; it dates from the 13th century. In a part of the remaining Abbey buildings, now used as a stable, one finds a tiny oriel window of unusual kind, having little Gothic lights full of diamond-shape panes, and a stone roof beautified by moss and lichen.

At the end of the main street stands the fine Parish Church, built of flints with stone dressings, in the Perpendicular style with its impressive embattled and pinnacled tower, with a chiming clock. In a canopied niche over the door is a statue of the Virgin. The interior is interesting and well-worth seeing, as it has been so little changed for centuries. There remain the high-backed pews ; a notably handsome carved pulpit dating from 1640, with a sounding board ; a pew for the clerk just below the pulpit, and a rood screen that has been restored.

Collectors of epitaphs will doubtless make a note of that to the memory of the little son Joseph, of George and Edith Summers who died in 1702, which runs as follows :

> " A little time did blast my pride
> And brought me hether ;
> The fairest flower within an hour
> May fade and wether."

Quaint and picturesque in several ways as Cerne is, one leaves with the impression that not only has it passed its prime, but that it is, one might almost say, undergoing a process of slow disintegration. Its streets so obviously belong to an age that has passed away. Few of its houses are similar in architecture, some are stone-roofed ; some tiled ; and, even nowadays, a few are thatched. But, though one cannot deny it a degree of picturesqueness and interest, it is what some writers would describe as ' a dead town,' though artists do and will find many little pictures in the old-world bow windowed shops ; old time houses ; the Abbey farmhouse at the end of the street in which the Church stands ; and along the banks of the little River Cerne.

But it is to see the Cerne Giant, on Giant's Hill, cut in the chalk close to the village that many people come. It is an enormous figure of a man, some two hundred feet in height, with gigantic fingers seven feet in length, and his club one hundred and twenty feet in length. Round the figure many legends have been woven, but nothing definite has been discovered regarding its origin or date. All the villagers, however, are certain it is very ancient.

One story, current years ago, was that a giant once actually lived in the neighbourhood, and oftentimes robbed the farmers of the Blackmoor Vale of their stock ; and that, following one of his raids, he had eaten too much and lay down to sleep on the side of the hill. Finding their enemy sound asleep, the villagers tied him with ropes, which they pegged down, killed him, and then cut the silhouette of the monster in the grass, and afterwards were able to cut out the turf to resemble a passable figure.

By some antiquarians, however, the view is taken that it was the work of the monks of Cerne Abbey. And one suggestion has been made, connecting the mysterious " Cross in Hand," on the bleak upland nearby, with the legend of the " Lost Pyx " of Hardy's well-known poem, and that it was the dying Giant that the priest of the legend rose up in the night to go and shrive. But no one knows anything definite about the matter. Only that the figure has been there ' time out of mind.'

It is worth while to go from Cerne Abbas to Maiden Newton, which Hardy calls Chalk Newton. It may be remembered *Tess of the D'Urbervilles* on leaving the village after breakfast, cut off her eyebrows in order to disguise herself. It also is the scene of *Interlopers at the Knap* in *Wessex Tales*.

One passes through some charming scenery to reach Maiden Newton though the two places are so little a distance apart. Those who remember the ancient *White Hart Inn*, (pulled down some years ago,) with its thatched roof, mullioned windows and gateway to the Yard, will regret its loss. It is replaced by an ordinary wayside inn of a modern and archi-tecturally uninteresting type.

But there is a picturesque mill ; and a church with a good deal of Norman work to attract one, charmingly situated, where a vine climbs over the old porch, and the churchyard is usually a garden of flowers ; an example to many seen in my wanderings, where neglect has resulted in a depressing wilder-ness. When last there, roses of all colours were climbing up the walls between the windows.

The church occupies the site of an old Saxon chapel, and the architecture of the present building is chiefly Perpendicular, though with surviving Norman work. There is a fine, embattled central tower, and interesting records going back to the middle half of the sixteenth century, and with some enlightening entries relating to Commonwealth times.

To gain some idea of the charm of a Wessex port and seaside resort, it is well worth while to go from Maiden Newton, by way of Beaminster, to Bridport, Port Bredy of the novels, and the scene of several of the Wessex tales ; of incidents in *Tess of the D'Urbervilles*, and particularly *The Mayor of Casterbridge*.

Douglas Snowdon.

Beaminster.   "Emminster"

By way of Toller Whelme to Beaminster one has fine views, and sees the town resting as it were in a great green hollow, and in the distance the heights of Lewesdon (900 ft.) and Pilsdon Pen. The town gives one an impression of modernity without aggressively modern houses, is also a tidy town and has a few thatched cottages and other relics of the past. Most of the houses are of a nice tint of yellowy-brown stone, with tiled roofs and exhibiting a pleasing variety as regards their architecture. And that pleasant feature (bow-windows) gives many of them character.

There is a fine and ancient Inn, the White Hart ; much frequented I gathered by those with agricultural interests, and by farmers. And there is a humble little square.

The townsfolk are proud of their church, and well may be ; for it is a magnificent building. Of which readers of *Tess of the D'Urbervilles* may remember the father of Angel Clare was Vicar. It dates from 1520, and possesses a wonderful tower of a rich golden-brown hue, which colour is, indeed, the dominating feature of the town. How numerous are its pinnacles, gargoyles, niches and other ornamentations no one can tell, and some of the carving is of remarkable delicacy and beauty. Chief among the subjects treated are the Blessed Virgin, the Crucifixion and the Ascension. Beautiful work that deserves inspection and study. As is the case of several Wessex churches one can recall, however, it is the tower and not the church as a whole, or the interior that enchants one.

Beaminster it will be discovered, is in a region of delightful manor houses dating from Tudor times onwards. Among the most notable is Mapperton, embosomed in a lovely glen. It is one of the famous houses of Wessex, and in the reign of Henry VIII the manor was in the possession of one Robert Morgan, who, it is recorded, by reason of " diverse infirmities could not without his grete daungier go without a head covering." And so the King " in tendre consideration thereof . . . . licensed him to use and were his bonnet on his hede at al tymys, as well in our presence as elsewher, at his Libertie." It was this Robert Morgan, having "diverse infirmities in his hedde," who built Mapperton, of grey stone, two storied and with dormer windows in its roof. And in those days we are told the following praiseworthy aphorism was inscribed in the Great Hall, saying of his wife and himself :—

> " What they spent, that they lent :
> What they gave, that they have :
> What they left, that they lost."

It is a house of many gables, charming bay windows, and possesses the undoubted attractiveness that comes from well-preserved age.

One comes upon Bridport along a pleasant gradually descending road, that follows the course of the River Brit at a short distance, until the latter eventually unites with the River Mangerton soon afterwards to fall into the sea. The town has little of antiquarian interest although of ancient origin, but, in the reign of Edward the Confessor, possessed a mint, a Priory of monks, and was of some size. It became a Royal demesne in the time of Henry III, who granted it a Charter. But its first municipal charter did not come until the reign of Henry VIII. The town today has two main streets ; that in which the Town Hall stands is unusually wide, and gives an air of spaciousness and of quiet prosperity to it. The port was a half-century or so ago engaged in the timber trade with Norway ; but of recent times this has been declined owing chiefly to two main causes, the employment of larger vessels, and the silting up of the harbour, but still has a coasting trade.

For centuries it has been noted for its hemp manufacture, and in days of sails furnished most of the rope for the Royal Navy, as well as making sail-cloth, fishing nets and twine of various kinds.

Douglas Snowdon

West Bay, Bridport.

"Port Bredy".

At one time, the story goes, the town supplied all the rope for hanging those condemned to death, and this gave rise to the curious saying of being " Stabbed with a Bridport dagger," so describing those who were hanged. Some years ago a Hampshire lady novelist, Miss Violet McFadden, used the phrase as the title for her interesting novel *A Bridport Dagger*.

The town's chief historical events have to do with the Civil War ; the Escape of Charles II after his defeat at Worcester ; and the Monmouth Rebellion. During the first named event, it was stormed by the Royalist forces, and changed hands several times.

In the second, King Charles II, when in flight, after the Battle of Worcester, had made for Trent House, the seat of the Wyndham family not far from Yeovil. There, adjoining Lady Wyndham's room, was a cleverly-constructed hiding chamber, of easy access in case of need. Here he lay concealed for some little time, until a number of Parliamentarian troopers came from Worcester into the neighbourhood in search of the King. It was then decided that the latter must leave.

He set out for Charmouth, where a boat to convey him across the Channel to France was thought to be in readiness. On his journey he had for companions Colonel Wyndham, and Miss Julian Coningsby, his cousin, who rode pillion behind the King, who was disguised as the servant of Colonel Wyndham.

Arrived at Charmouth it was found impossible to obtain a boat and so the party went on, almost immediately to Bridport, pursued by a Captain Macy, who was a Parliamentarian officer. On arrival at Bridport the royal party put up at the George Inn (pulled down some years ago), where the King, mistaken for an ostler by some soldiers, who had been at the Battle of Worcester, got into an altercation. After which risky incident Charles and his companions at once set out in flight along the Bridport to Dorchester road. They took a narrow by-way which is known as Lee Lane. At the corner of this, in the hedge, is a stone bearing the following inscription :—

KING CHARLES II
ESCAPED THROUGH THIS LANE
SEPT. XXIII, MDCLI.

Bridport is a rather charming place, with a hill with trees to serve as a background to the red-tiled and grey-stone roofs ; and the mere irregularity of the houses gives the place an attractive charm. In South Street, one passes on the way to the sea, the one time Castle Inn, with its stone-mullioned windows and handsome porch. The Harbour is known as West Bay, and is a strange little seaport, with a green verge in places merging with the shingle beach. The wooden piers are rather shaky looking, and the harbour itself is well-filled if three or four schooners of very moderate tonnage are in it, with a fishing boat or two and a very few rowing boats. But artists have found it a pleasant hunting ground for pictures, and the thatched cottages skirting the shingle beach add to the general effect. There is also an old-fashioned inn, the habitueès of which are of the seafaring type, and stray artists who find their way to West Bay in search of subjects.

Before turning back to Dorchester one may well include in one's itinerary Lyme Regis, which lies so close to the Devon border that some years ago an unsuccessful movement was initiated to have it transferred within the boundary of the latter county.

It is a delightful seaside resort of the quieter type with the little river Lym running through the town ; is picturesquely situated, it has romantic surroundings and a historic past. By approaching it along the Charmouth road one has a delightful first impression from the height one is above it ; especially from Timber Hill, ere one drops steeply into the little town, which from the high ground looks so small, viewed against the wide expanse of Lyme Bay and the Channel

Gateway Poxwell Hall

"Oxwell Hall."

beyond. It lies in a hollow at the mouth of the little River Lym or Buddle and its houses skirt the beach, and rise on the slopes of the two cliffs which shut it in on either side. These latter are well-known to geologists by reason of the many fossils found in them.

At the bottom of the steeply declining principal street there is a sea wall, which strikes the visitor as chiefly serving the purpose of preventing the houses slipping into the water!

Lyme Regis has been described as " a little town that does not know where it is going." Perhaps it may have been so when it was built, because even the main street deviously wanders on its way to the beach, and when this, and the promenade bordering the latter, is reached, known as the Marine Parade, one comes across an irregularity of houses that is one of the town's most attractive features. Indeed, many of the dwellings are both quaint and picturesque.

The chief building other that the Church, which seems to dominate the town when seen from the high ground above it, is the modern Town Hall built at the mouth of the Lym above the sea wall. Though only about half-a-century old the building has that air of detachment from any definite architectural scheme that characterises many another in the town.

The fossils found indicate that Lyme is without a shadow of doubt " an old, ancient place," as twenty-five feet or so of fossilised saurian, now in the Natural History Museum South Kensington, serves to prove. It was found more than a century ago by a Miss Mary Anning, a girl geologist, whose father kept a curiosity shop. She has surely made the greatest discovery, in that of the fossil of the Ichthyosaurus Platydon, that any young lady might hope for!

The town, therefore, has in a sense, a history going back, so scientists tell us, many thousands, if not millions of years. And Lyme is certainly known to have been a settlement in Saxon times, with a charter dating from Kynwulf, King of

Wessex. The addition of "Regis," to its original name, having been bestowed upon it by Edward I.

By the fourteenth century it had risen to some importance as a seaport and several times withstood the attacks of the French pirates, who, in 1554, were repulsed with great loss. And less than half-a-century later Lyme was able to furnish a couple of ships, the *Jacob* and *Revenge*, " with a good complement of men," to join the fleet prepared to resist the Spanish Armada.

On the outbreak of the Civil War between King Charles I and his Parliament, a little more than half-a-century later, Lyme was held for the latter by Sir Thomas Trenchard. Such importance was attached to the possession of the town by both the contending parties that Prince Maurice, in command of the Royalist forces in the West, determined to attack it. However, on calling upon the inhabitants to surrender he was, according to Clarendon, met with " so peremptory a refusal . . . that his Highness resolved not to attack."

Next year, however, he laid siege to the town, which was defended by Colonel Seeley and Lieutenant Colonel Robert Blake, who subsequently became the most famous of Admirals of Cromwellian days. The town was very fiercely attacked, and, in an account of the siege, we are told, " shots from demi-cannon, and culverins were fired into the town, together with grenados, fire-arrows, and divers balls of wild-fire, so that houses were burned down, and breaches blown through walls."

The town was, however, so stoutly defended that the siege lasted from April 10th till June 15th, 1644. The defenders at last appealed urgently for help, as both ammunition and provisions were running short, and Cromwell sent the Earl of Essex, with a large force to raise the siege. Prince Maurice, hearing that the Earl had reached Dorchester, abandoned his attempt on the town and marched towards Bristol.

The next historical event of importance affecting Lyme occurred forty-one years later, almost to a day, when one morning early risers on the Cobb, and a shepherd tending his flock on a hill above the town, were perturbed to see three ships steering for the port across the Bay, showing no colours to tell their nationality. The town was aroused; and the Mayor, Gregory Alford, gave orders for the drums to be beaten to give the alarm.

Soon boats could be seen being lowered and shortly after they were seen approaching. As they drew inshore, a tall figure, who wore a hat with black ostrich feathers in it, and was dressed in purple, and had a star on his breast, was seen seated in the stern of the first boat.

He landed with his companions, and it is recorded that they knelt and prayed on the beach for Divine aid in their enterprise, while at the same time a man raised and unfurled a banner on which were the words " Fear nothing but God." The spot where Monmouth landed is marked by a stone.

And so arrived the Duke of Monmouth, to claim a crown; and by failing ultimately to pay for his adventure with his life.

The Duke and his supporters marched to the Market Place, and here it was he proclaimed the object of his coming. The townsfolk were won over by his speech; and soon the countryside was ringing with the cry of " A Monmouth! a Monmouth!

Amidst great enthusiasm men flocked to his standard, but they were not the men that the Duke had been led to believe would be eager to support his claim to the throne. When he left Lyme he had gathered, it is said, less than 3,000 horses, and 2,000 foot (though much larger numbers are stated by some authorities) with which to defeat the army of his uncle King James II, which was soon on the move to meet him. On his march westward in the hope of raising the West Country, Monmouth gathered a few thousand more. But he was bitterly disillusioned ere he reached the fatal field of Sedgemoor, in Somerset, where less than a month later, on July 6th, 1685, he and his so-called army were utterly defeated.

Then followed Judge George Jeffrey's " Bloody Assize " at Dorchester, where more than a dozen Lyme Regis men and boys were condemned to death, and were subsequently executed in their home town.

Since the Monmouth Rebellion the history of Lyme has been uneventful, and little of its trade of former times, particularly that with Morlaix in Brittany, now remains.

Its prosperity, indeed, nowadays is not to any considerable extent derived from its port ; nor from any very active commercial development. Its efforts as a town are rather more concentrated to attract visitors and become a seaside holiday resort of the quieter type.

Its famous Cobb or stone pier is one of its chief attractions ; and its coast scenery is varied and in places very colourful and pretty. The Cobb, which is semi-circular in form, and of very considerable length, one is told, owing to its shape, possesses a peculiar characteristic in that voices and other sounds are heard along it, somewhat after the nature of the Whispering Gallery in St. Paul's Cathedral.

The Parish Church of St. Michael, originally a 15th century one, was carefully restored in 1855. A not altogether unsuccessful attempt was then made to re-create the original building which had been considerably spoiled by previous restorations. It is a good example of Perpendicular work, which has been to some extent, as it were, grafted on to the very old tower of the 15th century church. The vestry and vestibule are part of the old nave. At the western end of the church is a Norman arch. The Jacobean pulpit with a sounding-board is worth noting ; as is also the gallery of the same period. The pulpit was the gift of Richard Harvey, one of the merchant-adventurers of Lyme, who became a London mercer. On the west wall there is a fine piece of tapestry, said to represent the marriage of Henry Tudor with Elizabeth of

York; the gift of a former Vicar of Rousdon. There is also an interesting and old double Lectern, to which are chained Old and New Testaments, and a Prayer Book. The first, a Breeches Bible, is worth noting. There are also some fine stained glass windows. One to Miss Mary Anning, the geologist, who discovered the fossil saurian.

Lyme Regis had the beginning of its vogue as a seaside resort in the early years of the last century. And soon the little town with its pleasant surroundings, equable climate, and pretty scenery became the resort of literary people of note. Mary Russell Mitford, the author of *Our Village*; and of *Rienzi* and other plays, spent a considerable portion of her girlhood here. And somewhat later, Jane Austen, the author of *Pride and Prejudice*, and *Sense and Sensibility* paid Lyme Regis visits, and stayed in a large white cottage at the harbour end of the little promenade.

In all probability she wrote at least some portions of her novels there. And in her novel *Persuasion* gives vivid descriptions of the town, the surrounding countryside, and local characters which were more or less transcripts from life. " Bay Cottage " claims to be the original of Captain Harville's house. And Miss Constance Hill in her book dealing with Jane Austen's Homes, who interviewed the landlady of the cottage, tells us " the landlady talked of the Harvilles, the Musgroves, Anne Elliot and Captain Wentworth, as though they had been here but the season before. And pointing to a bedroom, exclaimed, ' That is the room where the poor young lady was nursed.' "

About half-way along the Cobb is what is considered the identical spot selected by Jane Austen from which Louisa Musgrove made her fatal leap.

It was Pinhay, a short distance westward along the coast that so entranced Jane Austen by its scenery, of which she wrote enthusiastically. She expresses her delight with the " green chasms between romantic rocks . . . . where is a scene so wonderful and so lovely." Here the serious landslip of 1839, when some forty acres or more of land moved to a lower level, and cottages and fields were transported bodily, has served to still further increase the picturesqueness, Jane Austen described.

In past times Lyme Regis was notable for its smugglers and trade in contraband with Morlaix in Brittany. Indeed, one of the most quaint and picturesque parts of Lyme architecturally is to be discovered along the banks of the Lym or Buddle River, just before it enters the sea. "Spanned by several arches, on which portions of houses have been built, and with many of the old ones nearly touching one another across the stream, with overhanging stories leaning towards each other . . . . . . "

Here it was, so I have been told, that the bold smugglers had their lairs, bringing the goods up the sinister-looking and trickling stream, and then hoisting them to places of safety in the houses above, or stowing them in the cellars.

The road back to Dorchester may be taken by way of Bridport along the ridge of hills to Askerswell with fine views of the sea and countryside, and thence to Winterborne Abbas. One of the group of Winterborne villages hereabouts, the name being derived from the little streams which flow only in winter time.

A slight divergence south-eastward from Winterborne Abbas will take one to the wonderful ancient earthwork, or encampment of Maiden Castle already described. And then by a minor road to join the main Weymouth-Dorchester highway.

CHAPTER VII

THE SCENES AND STORIES OF
SOME REPRESENTATIVE
NOVELS

A S IS, PERHAPS NATURAL, Dorchester plays an important part in a considerable number of the novelist's stories. The immediately surrounding country, indeed, lends itself admirably to the descriptive gifts that Hardy possessed in so marked a degree.

It is not my purpose to deal with the whole of the series of novels, into which a final edition and short stories have been gathered. From considerations of space, too, one is compelled to make only a selection; as representative as possible, but not laying claim, however, either to the selection or inclusion of the most excellent of Hardy's works in every case. And including only those the action of which is chiefly within the confines of Hardy's Wessex, or, say, Dorset.

It is with the identification of some of the more famous scenes in the novels chosen, and the description and illustration of the actual places as Hardy describes them that I have sought to deal.

The scenes of several of the novels, readers, will remember, overlap, as is the case with *The Trumpet Major* and *The Well Beloved ;* and with *The Mayor of Casterbridge, Tess of the D'Urbervilles*, and *Far from the Madding Crowd*.

Although Hardy studied his characters and their backgrounds so carefully that identification of the latter is a matter of no great difficulty to one well-acquainted with the localities in which the scenes are laid, he, on occasions, availed himself of the novelist's privilege to idealise them, and even in some cases to combine two or more places in one description. Taking certain details from one, and other characteristics from another.

For example, the Welland House—Lady Constantine's home—of *Two on a Tower* is partly Charborough House, near Warborne (Wimborne) and partly an old mansion (now a farm house), near Milborne St. Andrew's (Millpond St. Jude's).

In like manner, the column, or tower of the story, which plays so important a part in the novel, is, as Hardy tells us, in his preface to the novel " drawn in the main from the tower which stands within half-a-mile of Charborough and is in the Tuscan order of classic architecture." While as regards situation Hardy's description is taken from an obelisk called locally " Milborne Speer," or " King's Hill Speer," which stands on a circular and isolated hill, anciently an earthwork, amidst trees, and is situated north of Tolpuddle. Mid-way between Bere Regis and Puddletown on the Wareham to Dorchester road.

Hardy took the same sort of liberty with Talbothays dairy in *Tess of the D'Urbervilles*. Referring to the identification of this place, Hardy once wrote to the writer saying that Talbothays represented " two or three dairies in the Frome Valley . . . . and any existing house of that name has been so called since the novel was written." But subsequently, when cycling with him, we came to a dairy in the locality, which he admitted he had had in mind when describing Talbothays. It certainly possessed a number of features to be found in the description of the place in his novel.

Dorset has a trace of the Roman occupation still left in its idioms and in the faces of its peasantry ; of the ecclesiastic Saxon times in its buildings and traditions ; of the Norman period in many of its customs, and of the Middle Ages in much of its placidity and " behind the times air." Many of the old towns are still Roman in character as regards their plan, while examples of Elizabethan and early Georgian architecture still abound throughout the county in manor houses (many singularly well preserved) and in the townlets and villages.

It is not, however, in legends alone that one meets in Wessex with the England of the past, that seems to be almost still the England of the present to the traveller and wayfarer who journeys through Dorset and other parts of Wessex, with open eyes and in a romantic spirit. On all sides—in the names of the villages and hamlets scattered in the fertile vales or perched on some hill which, from its configuration, suggests the " earthworks " of the period of Roman occupation, rather than hillocks of nature's formation ; in the ruins of monastic institutions scattered thickly throughout the countryside ; in the churches, Saxon and otherwise such as the old Saxon Church at Shaftesbury (Shaston), where St. Edward was buried, and in the slow, old-time speech of the peasantry— the same almost mediæval spirit still in some measure persisting.

" Dorset stood still for several hundred years " is not the exaggerated statement of the antiquarian who made it, but a perhaps singular but scarcely exaggerated truth. However, much some may be inclined to dispute it.

* * * * *

THE TRUMPET MAJOR

The first book selected for illustration, deals with an older period of Dorset life than any other of Hardy's novels— if we exclude the shorter stories—and yet the speech of the characters in the comparatively modern Tess, which cannot be post-dated more than half-a-century, probably considerably less, is that of those in *The Trumpet Major* dealing with events in the early days of the century, when the South of England was under arms awaiting the threatened Napoleonic invasion. And children, if not their elders, lay a-bed o' nights trembling at the thoughts of the redoubtable " Boney." But doubtless, had there been a Hardy writing in the century before, the dialect of his types would have been but little different from that of today.

In each of the Wessex novels the reader is kept within a definite sphere of interest. In *The Trumpet Major* that sphere is practically comprised within a radius of ten or fifteen miles around Budmouth Regis (the Weymouth of today). In his preface the novelist states that this particular " tale is founded more largely on testimony—oral and written—than any other in this series."

And the relics in the way of trenches dug on the summits of the downs, old pike heads found in lofts, and volunteer uniforms preserved in clothes-presses of old-fashioned folk, are by no means a thing entirely of the past in Dorset.

Not many years ago, indeed, during the repairs of a warehouse on the Quay, Poole (Havenpool) the upper shutters of the loft were discovered to be drilled for musketry, and in a chest were found the sabretaches, uniforms and hats of the Poole volunteers of the time when invasion by Napoleon Bonaparte was hourly expected by the inhabitants of the coasts of Sussex, Hants and Dorset more especially. The fisher lads, who put on these now moth-eaten trappings so long ago, little realised the romance that attached to each brass button and each inch of cloth.

The Budmouth Regis of the present day, differs, no doubt, materially from the watering-place at which George III disported himself to the wonder, astonishment and admiration of the countryside round about. But the outlying villages of Overcombe (Upwey and Sutton), Kingsbere (Bere-Regis),

Sutton Poyntz.
Overcombe

Oxwell (Poxwell) are still very much what they were then, and have altered unappreciably since fair Anne Garland threw down her work on that fine summer morning to watch the soldiers assembling on top of the down above Overcombe Mill.

Indeed, after reading the story on the spot one can realise to the full the consternation of the villagers lest these un-looked-for soldiers should indicate that Bonaparte had out-witted the fleet cruising in the Channel, and had attacked timorous Budmouth on the flank.

Overcombe Mill, where Hardy made Anne Garland and her mother live, still grinds (like those of the gods) slowly if exceedingly small ; and the miller of today, if not a Loveday by descent, might well pass for one. The "Lookout," to which several of the characters in the story made anxious pilgrimage in search of signs of the French invaders is still so known locally, and the troublous times which gave rise to such things are permanently recorded by the name of Kimmeridge "Lookout," a few miles farther down the coast.

A succession of the least humorous and successful scenes in the story are those in Chapter XII, in which is recorded, " How everybody, great and small, climbed to the top of the Downs."

We are told that it was on " a clear day, with little wind stirring, and the view from the downs, one of the most extensive in the county, was unclouded. The eye of any observer who cared for such things swept over the wave-washed town, and the bay beyond, and the isle, with its pebble bank, lying on the sea, like a great, crouching animal, tethered to the mainland."

It is a scene like this which, happily, in many instances, yet remains immutable in Wessex. The isle " crouches " today as it did then ; " the wave-washed town " still preserves some of its early-in-the-century air, and when once away on the sloping uplands to the north east, out of earshot of fashionable talk and the sight of present day toilettes and ubiquitous bicycles and motor cars, one can almost imagine that the soldiers of the German Legion and York Hussars of those days, as Hardy describes them in " white buckskin pantaloons, three-quarter boots, scarlet shakos set off with lace, mustachios, waxed to a needle point, and, above all, those richly ornamented blue jackets mantled with the historic pelisse " are still patrolling the street of the distant town, or guarding the matutinal bathing of his Majesty King George the Third.

" At twelve o'clock," we are told in the story, " the review, that had been taking place, was over, and the King and his family left the hill. The troops then cleared off the field, the spectators followed, and by one o'clock the downs were again bare." The white horse and rider, one of the several cut in the chalk downs and uplands of England, now an object of curiosity to tourists and visitors to Budmouth, and a landmark for those who go down to the sea in ships, was not there in those days. It was an artistic afterthought to commemorate the event, and King George's visit.

The harbour has not so greatly altered since sailor Bob Loveday on the morning of September the third, long ago, after the renunciation of the girl he loved in favour of soldier John, returned from the barracks to Budmouth, " passed on to the harbour, where he remained awhile, looking at the scene of unloading and loading craft, and swabbing of the decks of yachts ; at the boats and barges rubbing against the quay wall, and at the houses of the merchants, some ancient structures of solid stone, some green-shuttered with heavy bow-windows, which appeared as if to drop into the harbour by their own weight."

Almost the only difference today is the presence of steamers, which have, doubtless, driven some of the barges away. But the houses, the quay, the stores and the old stone bridge are still there, as in Loveday's time.

The Isle of Portland—no true island now or then, but a peninsula—has altered even less. Anne Garland might still set out, as it is related in *The Trumpet Major*, from Overcombe, and after finishing her shopping in Budmouth itself, cross the ancient bridge, and take her way to Portland through the old town along the coast road. Today she would be, as then, confronted, before reaching the base of Portland Hill, by the steep street of Wells, dotted with houses, raised tier upon tier, so that the doorstep of one man is sometimes almost on a level with the chimney of his neighbour immediately below.

From the bare promontory of the " Bill " we can look upon the same prospect as when Anne watched Nelson and Hardy's *Victory*, with Bob Loveday aboard her, and the *Euryalus* frigate, in her wake, sail clean out of sight down the Channel.

This desolate isle with the wonderful pebble beach linking it to the mainland and stretching for some fifteen miles in an unbroken curve toward Bridport to the west, and encircling the famous West Bay, is much the same as when Anne Garland, watching the last topmast of the *Victory* sink below the distant horizon, murmured, without removing her wet eyes from the vacant and solemn horizon, " They that go down to the sea in ships, that do business in great waters . . . ," and turned, at the sound of another voice completing the verse, to find the vanished Bob Loveday's brother John at her elbow.

* * * * *

FAR FROM THE MADDING CROWD

In this novel Thomas Hardy has written a story almost exclusively of the farm. And it is no small tribute to his genius that he can enlist his readers' sympathies so completely in its every-day life, which is bounded, one might with tolerable accuracy say, by the lambing season in the spring, and the getting in of root crops in the autumn.

The contrasts of character in the book are sharper than in several of the Wessex novels. A more clean-cut divergence than that afforded by the vicious adventurer, Sergeant Troy, and the unselfish, plodding, dog-faithful Gabriel Oak, the shepherd, it would not be easy to imagine. Troy with his cheap gallantry and echo of town ways, his power over women, with whom he came in contact, by both physical and mental means (as an example of the former there is the wonderful sword-play bewitchment of Bathsheba in the ferny hollow, when he severs a lock of hair from her head ; and of the latter his veneer of education and flattering talk) ; and Gabriel Oak with his stolid ways and countryside sympathies.

And the same applies to the women characters also. Fanny Robin, the dazzled and deceived, serving as a foil to the trustful, ignorant Bathsheba equally dazzled, but at first cautious.

Though tragedy and comedy alternate in the pages of the novel, the tragic consequences of Sergeant Troy's amours are in a measure set off by the excellent rustics and their delicious humourous talk. But it is the tragic note which predominates. For the fate of Fanny is not less insistent than the pen of the novelist would have it, and the marriage of the long-suffering Gabriel Oak with Bathsheba, in the last few pages, does not succeed in effacing from the memory the tragic doing to death of Troy by Boldwood in the hall of his own house.

The scene of the story is circumscribed, as is the case with most of Hardy's novels. It centres in Weatherbury (Puddletown) a village some six miles distant from Casterbridge ; and within a radius of a few miles of this Wessex hamlet, the whole action of the tale takes place.

Many of the descriptions of rural life are charming, and conjure up as accurate an idea of the *locale* as would be afforded by an etching. One of the most important scenes in the book —the sheep-washing—affords an instance of this. It is a good example of the care and accuracy with which the novelist literally builds up his descriptions of even unimportant places. The true artistic economy of words is evident in every phrase. Boldwood, Shepherd Gabriel Oak, Jan Coggan and the other farm hands were there, and Bathsheba was looking on. " The river," we are told, " slid along noiselessly as a shade, the swelling reeds and sedge forming a flexible palisade along its moist bank. To the north of the mead were trees . . . . . "

Though this might serve as a general description of numberless Wessex meads, and the streams running silently through them, yet a distinct vision of this particular mead on Bathsheba's farm, called Weatherbury Upper Farm actually Lower Waterston, is clearly brought before the reader's eyes.

Nowhere, probably do fairs survive with more pertinacity in the South and South-west of England than in Wessex. And if one may believe the word of the country folk, who have attended them from days of childhood to those of hoary old age, the surviving fairs differ little from those of five decades or more ago.

Ever on the alert to make use of existing circumstances in his novels indicative of the placidity of life, disturbed only occasionally by such things, as Fairs, it is little to be wondered at that Hardy should have fixed upon one of the most noted of these gatherings for description. Greenhill (Woodbury Hill) Fair, held in September, is known throughout the countryside. There he sets several vivid scenes in *Far from the Madding Crowd*. To it come shepherds with their flocks of South Downs, Leicesters, old West of England horned breeds, and even Exmoors, with parti-coloured faces and legs.

The fair is held on the summit of a hill standing about half-a-mile outside Kingsbere (Bere Regis). Antiquarians are of the opinion that the hill, up whose crumbling sides the two main roads leading to the top wind, is the site of an ancient British encampment ; for at the summit there is a huge rampart and entrenchment, oval in form, and within the confines of this the Fair takes place. There are a few hovels and cottages of a permanent character on the crest of Greenhill, as in Hardy's time ; but most of those who fore-gather for the fairing are content to be under canvas or in gipsy, and now-adays motor caravans.

Down the centre of this temporary encampment, running almost north and south, the main street of the Fair is made on either side of which stand the booths and stalls—the former abodes of thin men, fat women, two-headed calves ; the latter till very recent times laden with ginger-bread and cheap, gaily-coloured china ornaments, with which shooting galleries, " cokernut shies " and nine-pins contest popularity.

There is an interesting custom in connection with the Fair. On an appointed day a small band of gipsies gather on the hill in order to sign some deed or paper, and it is said, if ever this is not done the right to hold a fair lapses and is for ever lost.

The old drovers, commoner ten years ago than now throughout Wessex, are another survival of Greenhill. Early in the morning of the first day of the Fair we are told that " nebulous clouds of dust (are) to be seen floating between the pairs of hedges in all directions. These gradually converged upon the base of the hill, and the flocks became individually visible, climbing the serpentine way which led to the top. Thus, in slow procession, they entered the openings to which the roads wended."

This is almost as true of the Greenhill Fair of compara-tively recent times, as of the Fair more than half-a-century ago, when Hardy wrote the novel. When I visited it last the circus which plays so important a part in Troy's reappearance, and in his wife Bathsheba's subsequent history, was almost like its prototype of the story, and one could almost imagine that Troy was giving his sensational performance of Dick Turpin inside. Now, as then, everybody for miles round goes to Greenhill. The better-class farmers patronising the first day, and the

Puddletown

"Weatherbury."

SNOWDON

second day being more or less given over to the labourers, their wives, sweethearts, sons and daughters.

Troy after his marriage with Bathsheba goes to America and gains a living as a teacher of boxing and fencing. On his return to England he takes up with the circus life again, and arrives at Greenhill Fair. Troy finds that Bathsheba is engaged to Boldwood, a farmer, who is her neighbour. Troy wishes Bathsheba to go with him, and Boldwood who had long wished to marry Bathsheba shoots Troy. He was tried for murder and sentenced to death, afterwards reprieved. Bathsheba then marries Gabriel Oak, a local farmer. Her wedding in Weatherbury Church (Puddletown) is described by Hardy as " the most private, secret, plainest wedding that it is possible to have."

From the time of Greenhill Fair and Troy's reappearance the story moves with rapidity to its close. The jail in which Boldwood, the farmer, one of Bathsheba's most pertinacious lovers, was confined, waiting under sentence of death for execution, has since that time been pulled down and rebuilt after much more modern ideas, but the gateway is much the same as ever. And it is easy enough to enter into Gabriel Oak's feelings as he turned to look back at the jail (after saying goodbye to the condemned man, who was also his rival) and saw " the upper part of the entrance . . . . . and some moving figures "—these last placing in position the post of the gibbet to be used on the morrow.

One cannot help feeling that the true end of the story comes with the scene at midnight on the Casterbridge road, when Laban brought to Gabriel Oak and Jan Coggan, and the rest of the waiting villagers, who had walked toward Casterbridge from Weatherbury to meet him, the news of the murderer's reprieve.

The conventional ending, with " the most private, secret, plainest wedding that it is possible to have " of Bathsheba and Gabriel comes, indeed, almost as a dangerous anti-climax.

* * * * *

TESS OF THE D'URBERVILLES

Few, if any, of the Wessex novels attain to the supremacy of interest which *Tess of the D'Urbervilles* has for the general reader—vastly human, tragically idyllic as it is ; compact of the impulses of a woman of the soil, and a weak man's vacillations.

At the time of its first appearance the story aroused much discussion and comment, one critic at least regarding it erroneously, we should say—as a " manifestation of a new Hardy," rather than as an unusually marked and firmer development along one particular line of the novelist's preferences in his art. Although the novel is rather of the nature of a brief for the inexorableness of Fate than a story teaching one particular moral idea (as might, perhaps, be inferred, it is the novelist's intention, from the sub-title, " A Pure Woman Faithfully Presented "), it is painful with the stern reality of recorded facts rather than with that of so-called realism clumsily introduced.

The present writer always believed that Hardy never regarded Tess as a wanton, but as a woman of the soil, to use a common phrase " more sinned against than sinning." And indeed, the fact of the act of Tess abandoning Alec D'Urberville and returning to Angel Clare, her husband seems to my mind to support Hardy's view of her character.

But with all its onward march toward the end—at times one obtains a glimpse, as it were, of the inevitableness—the story fails to carry absolute conviction. The reader is tempted in reading the last few pages of the book to ask why, when Tess has once more succumbed to the evil influence of Alec D'Urberville, the murder is committed. This may appear hypercriticism ; but not for the first time in Tess's history does a motive assume an apparently shadowy and insufficient character.

With the main incidents of the story most of my readers will doubtless be familiar ; with the feckless, ne'er-do-well Durbeyfield and his haphazard wife and family ; with the incident of Alec D'Urberville's treachery (with which the real history of Tess may be said to commence) ; with Angel Clare and the life at Talbothays ; with the love of Tess for Angel, and her ultimate marriage with him ; with their almost immediate separation on the latter's discovery of his wife's former declension from virtue ; with Tess's struggle for subsistence (one of the finest parts of the novel) and faithfulness to her absent and non-communicating husband ; till the villian of the piece—Tess's " bad angel "—reappears in the person of Alec D'Urberville ; with the murder of the latter by Tess in the Sandbourne (Bournemouth) apartments ; with the coming of Clare, too late, as so often happens with men of his type in real life, as well as in fiction ; with the flight of the reunited husband and wife into Wessex ; with the capture of Tess at Stonehenge ; with the last scene, when Angel Clare and 'Liza-Lu watch with pain-contracted hearts the black emblem, denoting Tess's sudden plunge into eternity, flutter slowly, almost on the stroke of eight, up the bare staff on the tower of Wintoncester (Winchester) Jail.

Once or twice during the progress of the story the novelist seems to suggest—it is little more—that Tess's misfortunes and predilections are the outcome of heredity, and what are usually known as " the sins of the fathers." But it is scarcely possible to study the book in the light of hereditary consequences. There is too little indication of the life of her ancestors to allow one to trace heredity as clearly as one should to enable one to accept the conclusion of the book as, in the first place, inevitable, and in the second as accounted for by the theory of heredity.

The story opens with what may be describes as the undoing of John Durbeyfield (D'Urberville). Always lazy, he is destined to become more so by reason of the antiquarian

Parson Tringham's indiscretion in telling him he was in reality a descendant of the D'Urbervilles, and the possessor of grand and noble " skillentons " laid to rest in the family vault of Kingsbere (Bere Regis) Church. Information which turns lazy John into a dreamer of dreams, and a man disposed to make heavy drafts on the bank of former greatness to meet current expenses brought about by a large family and slender resources.

The scene where the Parson meets John Durbeyfield on the road to Marlott, as the latter is returning from the hill town of Shaston (Shaftesbury), is in the true Hardy vein ; a blend of the humourous, the pathetic and the ridiculous.

It is toward Shaston that Tess eventually takes her way in search of the grand relatives, of whom Mrs. Durbeyfield (her mother) hoped so much. The town is still so denominated on the ancient milestones, which stand on the road to it from Sturminster Newton. The more modern and usual name is Shaftesbury. It stands perched on a hill overlooking the beautiful Blackmoor Vale in which Tess had lived all her life ; and it is, if one may believe tradition, the site of more than one skirmish between King Alfred the Great and the Danes, and is, therefore, at least a thousand years old. It still contains many old houses, and the Church dates back well into the Norman period.

Along Shaston High Street Tess must have passed on her way from Marlott to Chaseborough (Cranborne), which lay to the south-east, on that early morning following the loss of the Durbeyfield horse, which proved the last straw, and broke up the huckstering business in which her father sought to gain a precarious livelihood when sober, and that precipitated the disorganisation of the family finances.

One can almost believe that the street has not altered a stone since Tess trod it on her way to seek aid of her suppositious relatives in their grand house, " The Slopes," where she was destined to suffer so much.

The third phase of Tess's story provides us with some of the best of the rural scenes contained in the novel. It is the second setting-out of the girl to relieve the pressure upon her family's ever-slender resources. The motive is the same as the first; but the inspiration, how different! Not any more were there fine ancestors or grand relatives in Tess's simple calculations; "there should be no more D'Urberville air castles in the dreams and deeds of the new life" which she was adopting. "She would be dairymaid Tess, and nothing more.

And so it was that "on a thyme-scented, bird-hatching morning in May" Tess set out, in a hired trap, "luggage and all, for Stourcastle (Sturminster Newton), through which it was necessary to pass on her journey" to Talbothays. "She went," we are told "through Stourcastle without pausing." Passing, doubtless, over the old bridge which lies at the bottom of the hill at the foot of the main street of the old-fashioned town; past the remains of the cross, along the street which has a wide commencement and a narrow ending.

Egdon Heath, beloved of the novelist, is afterwards crossed, and Tess, "after sundry wrong turnings . . . . . found herself on the summit commanding the long-sought-for-vale, the Valley of the Great Dairies," in which the most purely romantic phase of her chequered life was afterwards passed.

The courting of Tess by Angel Clare, after they had met as fellow-workers at Talbothays Dairy, is the least convincing portion of the vivid picture of the life led in this typical Wessex dairy farm.

But the drive in the thirtieth chapter is an excellent example of the skill with which the novelist contrives to suggest atmosphere, and the effect of the atmospheric conditions on his characters.

In the first few lines a description of Egdon Heath occurs, which, to those who have traversed its wide waste of broken moorland, conjures up a picture with a wonderful economy of words at once convincing and suggestive. It was likewise " in the diminishing daylight that (we) went along the level roadway through the meads, which stretched away into grey miles, and were backed in the extreme edge of the distance by the swarthy and abrupt slopes of Egdon Heath. On its summit stood clumps and stretches of fir-trees, whose notched tips appeared like battlemented towers crowning black-fronted castles of enchantment."

The railway station toward which Angle Clare and Tess were bound with the full milk cans in the cart on this particular evening is still as then, a friction point in the iron chain which serves to link Wessex and its dairy farms with the outer world, of which the inhabitants knew so little. And the holly bush under which Tess sheltered is still there, and has, doubtless, since afforded a like scant comfort to other dairymaids who have made similar journeys in the rain.

It was during this memorable ride that Tess attempted the thankless task of confessing to her lover her previous misfortune—a task made difficult by her own sense of disgrace and fear of losing him ; and rendered impossible by the spirit of raillery with which Angel Clare received her opening sentences. The spirit of aloofness—which characterised all Clare's and Tess's love-making—still seemed to exist as "they drove on through the gloom, forming one bundle inside the sail cloth, the horse going as he would, and the rain driving against them."

And notwithstanding the suggestion conveyed by the words, " the appetite for joy " which may be held to hint a reason for Tess's consenting to marry Clare ; the motive other than that afforded by an almost furtive expression of affection, remains to the general reader shadowy.

Tess is soon afterward married. And Clare, who has decided to make himself acquainted with milling, carries her off to Wellbridge (Wool), at which place is the flour mill where he had elected to gain his experience.

Wool. Bridge House.
"Wellbridge" House

By a singular coincidence the house in which he had taken rooms, is a portion of a fine old manorial residence, once belonging to the D'Urberville family, now, since its partial demolition, a farmhouse. A grey-reddish pile standing amid the meads, with modern excrescences in the way of outbuildings, and a cottage or two, attached to its own fading glories, and with the weed-grown Frome, thick with rushes along its banks, almost washing its garden wall.

We are told that the newly married pair after leaving, for their honeymoon " drove by the level road along the valley for a distance of a few miles, and reaching Wellbridge, turned away from the village to the left, and passed over the great Elizabethan bridge which gives the place half its name."

It needs no very great stretch of the imagination, when one stands on the bridge, to conjure up the scene as the broken-down conveyance, a relic of post-chaise days, with its juvenile postillion of sixty-odd years, lumbered up to the little wicket which admitted them to the bare patch of garden surrounding the house. We can see in imagination, these two walk along the narrow path to the porched doorway, with its bench recessed on either side, and enter the house which was to become the scene of the wrecking of Tess's happiness.

On the landing the portraits of the two " horrid women," which so alarmed poor Tess, still stare at the casual visitor ; and the bridal chamber, large, uneven of floor and lighted by narrow stone mullioned windows, remains, we fancy, much as it was then, except for the addition of a garish modern wall-paper.

In this gloomy house with its mouldy greatness, Thomas Hardy found a fitting and a singularly appropriate setting for the mutual confessions of Angel Clare and his wife. The different value that society is pleased to set upon the sin as between man and woman is not insisted upon ; but, with consummate art, it becomes the inevitable value in this particular case. The weakness of the man's character; and the piteous trust and frailty of the woman stand out, clear-cut and convincing.

We feel Tess's loneliness as, after their mutual confessions, Clare, closing the door softly behind him, goes out into the blackness of the night, well-matching in its sinister gloom his own thoughts. The dog-faithfulness of Tess, who follows Clare at a distance, dumb with pain on becoming devastatingly aware of that " cruelty of fooled honesty (which) is often greater after enlightment," and that such feeling was overwhelming her husband now, is brought clearly to the reader's mind. The immense folly of the man is brought out subtly, but with ever-increasing clearness, during every yard of that night's walk, and in the conversation and attitude of Clare on their return to the house.

Their life during the few succeeding days before they part, Clare to go abroad and Tess to return to her old home, is described in detail. The man takes his way daily to Wellbridge Mill and the woman waits in the gloomy house eating her heart out in sorrow, and devising wild schemes by which she might put an end to herself, or by which her husband might rid himself of her.

At midnight, before they are to part, Tess, asleep in the upper chamber, awakes on hearing the noise of footsteps in the darkened farmhouse. Her door opens and she sees Angel Clare entering the room in the moonlight. At first a throb of joy possesses her, emanating from the thought that flashes into her brain—he has come to her with forgiveness.

But it is not so.

She soon realises that he is asleep, and that he thinks her dead.

But when he stoops over her and, taking her in his arms, creeps down the creaking staircase, and after leaving the house proceeds in the direction of the Mill and the ruins of the

Cistercian Abbey, away to the south, amid the trees, she makes no resistance. Half hoping that she and he will find an end to their troubles while crossing the river on the slender and now railless footbridge, by a heedless step on his part, which would plunge them into the swirling, foaming, weed-grown stream below.

At length " they reached the ruined choir of the Abbey-church. Against the north wall was the empty stone coffin of an abbott . . . . . In this Clare carefully laid Tess."

While standing looking into the strange stone coffin, furnished as it is with a slight access of breadth at the shoulders and a scooped-out hollow for the head, the traveller in Wessex can easily reconstruct the midnight scene as Clare, stooping beneath the boughs of the overhanging trees, laid white-robed Tess in the leaf-strewn resting place. On the day I last visited it the environing trees had rich autumn tints, and the thick canopy of foliage made the place little less gloomy than on the moonlight night of Tess's adventure.

Next day Tess and Angel Clare drove through Weather-bury (Puddletown) and Stagfoot Lane to Nuzzlebury (possibly Hazelbury Bryan) and on to Stourcastle, (Sturminster Newton), where they parted at the cross roads just outside the town. Clare to take his wide way in the world outside the confines of Wessex, and she to return to her home once more, and then to her struggle for existence at field work on the farm at Flint-comb Ash (near Nettlecombe Tout).

The story proceeds with the narration of her life on the farm ; her fruitless visit to her husband's home at Emminster (Beaminster) ; the reappearance of Alec D'Urberville ; the breaking up of Tess's old home ; the journey to Kingsbere in search of lodging ; and the temptation which Alec D'Urber-ville placed in her way, to which after a struggle she succumbed.

The Durbeyfield household, with their furniture, set out almost immediately after the father's death for Kingsbere,

" the spot of all spots in the world which could be considered the D'Urbervilles' home."

" Though they had started so early it was quite late in the afternoon when they turned the flank of an eminence which formed part of the upland called Greenhill . . . . just ahead of them was the half-dead townlet of their pilgrimage, Kingsbere, where lay those ancestors of whom her father had spoken and sung to painfulness "—the " skillentons " of those whose departed glories had so prejudicial an influence on the Durbeyfield family in general. The rooms they wanted were let ! "

This wandering family was therefore suddenly and unexpectedly confronted with the problem as to where they could repose for the night. " Her (Tess's) mother looked hopelessly at fault. ' What shall we do now, Tess ? ' she said bitterly. And then she summed up her stricken faith in these ancestors, who had never brought them any luck, but bad, in the sentence, ' Here's a welcome to your ancestor's lands ! ' "

The cart eventually pulled up under the churchyard wall, the homeless ones camped out under the four-post bedstead placed near the D'Urberville window, on the south side of the church. Inside the window " were the tombs of the family, covering in their dates several centuries. They were canopied, altar-shaped and plain ; their carvings being defaced and broken ; their brasses torn from the matrices, the rivet-holes remaining like marten-holes in a sand cliff . . . "

It is while Tess, who had crept in at the open door of the church, is gazing at and meditating upon this evidence of the fallen greatness of her family, that Alec D'Urberville makes his reappearance.

Having, during the time that Tess had parted from Angel Clare, become an " excellent fiery Christian man," and travelling the countryside preaching at camp meetings and in barns.

It is the beginning of the end. Shortly afterward the story finds Tess in apartments at Sandbourne (Bournemouth) again his mistress.

Angel Clare had by then returned from Brazil in ill-health, and was eagerly searching for Tess so that he might live with her and make amends. He hears that she is with Alec D'Urberville, and goes to the house "The Herons" where she is. Tess, maddened, by her position, stabs Alec, and like a hunted creature, Tess, in company with Clare, for some days eludes justice, which at last finds them on the Great Plain (Salisbury Plain), amid the weird circle of Stonehenge.

It is here, early in the morning, that the officers of the law, capture her as she is sleeping—a veritable Hardy touch this—on one of the immense stones of this sacrificial temple of past ages. As the police officers close in upon her "the eastward pillars and their architraves stood up . . . . against the light."

The actual end of the story is very rapid. Two pages or little more suffice. Tess is condemned to death and is confined in (Wintoncester) Winchester Jail.

Angel and Tess's sister 'Liza-Lu, journey to the city to see what of the end was vouchsafed to them. It was not much. They climbed the upward slope of the High Street, and passed to the top of the great West Hill, whence they gazed at the distant building, with the ugly flat-topped octagonal tower, in which the few remaining minutes of Tess's life were speeding away.

"Upon the cornice of the tower there was a tall staff. Their eyes were rivetted on it. A few minutes after the hour had struck something moved slowly up the staff and extended itself upon the breeze. It was a black flag."

"The two speechless gazers bent themselves down to the earth, as if in prayer . . . . . the flag continued to wave silently.

"Justice' was done, and the President of the Immortals (in Æschylean phrase) had ended his sport with Tess."

*   *   *   *

TWO ON A TOWER

In this novel we have a romance ; a book of a different calibre and importance from the foregoing. Here Thomas Hardy crosses the borders of his Wessex somewhat, and in the character of Lady Constantine he gives us a woman of the world in place of the rustic maidens " with primeval passions " in which the novelist takes especial delight. Swithin St. Cleeve, the young astronomer in whom Vivette, Lady Constantine, takes so deep an interest, is essentially a dreamer, and it speaks well for the skill of the narrator that Hardy arouses in the reader so satisfactory a curiosity concerning his doings. Lady Constantine herself is one more of those indiscreet, subtly emotional women among the feminine portraits of Hardy's gallery.

A woman at first so æsthetically interested in the beauty of the astronomical youth, whom she accidentally found in possession of the " tower " on her estate, as to simulate an enthusiasm which she did not feel for a science which she could not comprehend, and afterward to commit the indiscretion of allowing herself to fall in love with the lad, and seek to cover her great *faux pas* and legitimatise her and Swithin's child with true Wessex irony, by her marriage with a bishop !

The story opens with Lady Constantine's arrival, on a clear wintry afternoon, at the entrance to her domain, Welland House, situated a little off the old Melchester (Salisbury) road at Millpond St. Jude's (Milborne St Andrew's). She gazes at the surrounding country through the field gate, and her attention is riveted by, " the central feature of the middle distance . . . . a circular, isolated hill, of no great elevation . . . . covered with fir-trees." This hill " was yet further marked out from the general landscape by having on its summit a tower in the form of a classic column which, though partly immersed in the plantation, rose above the tree-tops to a considerable height." It was this tower (compounded of two such memorials, the other being situated near Charborough), that was destined to play so important a part in the history of Lady Constantine and Swithin St. Cleeve. It is now, owing to the growth of the surrounding trees, only possible to catch a glimpse of the column from a few stated points.

This " fir-shrouded hill-top," we are told, " was (according to some antiquaries) .... an old Roman Camp .... with the remains of an outer and inner vallum, a winding path leading up between their overlapping ends by an easy ascent .... "

It was up this ascent that the writer climbed to find, as so frequently happened during his pilgrimages in Wessex, the description of the book accurately fitting the actuality of nature. " The gloom and solitude which prevailed round the base were remarkable ; .... some boughs and twigs rubbed the pillar's sides or occasionally clicked in catching each other. The sob of the environing trees was here expressly manifest. Below the level of their summits the masonry was lichen-stained and mildewed, for the sun never pierced the moaning cloud of blue-black vegetation .... "

It was not for some months that Lady Constantine found an opportunity of visiting the spot which had aroused her curiosity on the afternoon of her homecoming. However, one day in February, she drove out and directed that the carriage should enter the gate of one of the fields surrounding the hill, and put her down as close to the base of the hill as possible. She climbed the outer slope of the old earthworks and entered the wood, prompted partially by curiosity and partially by a desire to vary the monotony of her curiously lonely and uninteresting life, by even so mild an adventuring. She discovered the doorway at the foot of the column, and finding it unfastened, pushed it open and ascended the staircase.

On the top she was brought face to face with the youthful astronomer, who at first is too occupied with the cyclone which he states is taking place in the sun to pay any attention to her presence ; even when she addresses him.

When he at length looks up, it is to be mutually enamoured, and it is with the history of these two persons, so strangely thrown together, that the story is concerned.

The main interest of the tale it is somewhat difficult to locate with exactness, the whole plot turning upon Lady Constantine's matrimonial experiment with Swithin—which proves to be a bigamous one, as her husband, Sir Blount, was still alive at the time—and her singular method of adjusting matters, and of saving her reputation by her ultimate marriage with the Bishop of Melchester.

Her death from heart failure on the day when she again meets Swithin, on his return from South Africa, whence he had gone to pursue his astronomical studies, is the method adopted for the disposal of a character as whimsical and elusive as any the novelist has created.

*   *   *   *

THE WELL BELOVED

The scene of this most elusive of our selected stories is to all intents and purposes laid in the extreme south of Wessex on the Isle of Slingers (Portland), with an occasional transference of the scene to London.

The Well Beloved, which has the illuminating sub-title of " A Sketch of a Temperament," is chiefly concerned with the doings of one Jocelyn Pierston, a successful sculptor, the son of a quarry owner, and with three generations of Avices—the first of whom was Avice Caro, the girl playmate of his childhood's days on the island, and the last, her granddaughter, and his dalliance with one Marcia Bencomb, with whom the vacillating Jocelyn philanders and eventually marries.

The novelist, in the preface to the standard edition of the book, gives the following explanation of the elusive character of the story, which without it would appear scarcely more than a shadowy puppet-show, and a peg on which to hang some fine and unsurpassed descriptions of the island scenery and atmospheric conditions in South Wessex.

" The peninsula, carved by time out of a single stone," we are told . . . . . " has been for centuries the home of a curious and almost distinctive people, cherishing strange beliefs and singular customs, now for the most part obsolete. Fancies, like certain soft-wooded plants which cannot bear the silent inland frosts, but thrive by the sea in the roughest of weather, seem to grow up naturally here, in particular among those natives who have no active concern in the labours of the ' isle.' Hence it is a spot apt to generate a type of personage like the character imperfectly sketched in these pages—a native of natives—whom some may choose to call a fantast . . . . but whom others may see only as one that gave object continuity and a name to a delicate dream."

This dream is, it may be remarked, the feminine *alter ego* of the man, but, after all, not merely that. The " well-beloved " is not only the other self, but the *ideal* other self, which even less often materialises to reward the most earnest of seekers of the other self.

Native born inhabitants of the peninsula are very proud of the fact, others are locally known as " Kimberlins."

The village of Portland lies on the landward side of the " Isle of Slingers " facing almost north-west. A conglomeration of houses and stone sheds built in tiers up the steep hillside. Above the highest towers, the green and then grey slope marking the summit. The main street of this townlet, which " is connected with the mainland by a long, thin neck of pebbles—unparalleled in its kind in Europe," is exceedingly steep, and leads into the centre of the once island, now peninsula, " that stretches out like the head of a bird into the English Channel."

It was up this Street of Wells (as it is called in the story) that Jocelyn Pierston on a summer afternoon climbed on his way to the eastern village. He was paying one of his periodical visits to his birthplace, which he had left in youth to become a sculptor. He felt warm and sat down opposite a cottage to rest. The whirr and rasping sound of the quarrymen and stone-sawyers at work came to him as he sat. A sound familiar enough in his boyhood, but now strange and familiar at one and the same time.

In the cottage at the corner of the lane on the left-hand of the northern entrance to Sylvania (Pennsylvania) Castle, lived a Mrs. Caro and her daughter Avice, the latter having been the playmate of his childhood. He enters the cottage, and while talking to her mother Avice herself makes her appearance ; and, notwithstanding that she has grown up (her age is about eighteen) and he has attained to man's estate she greets her returned playfellow with a kiss. Jocelyn gives a start of surprise, which escapes the girl, but not the eyes of her mother, who reproves her—" Avice—my dear Avice! Why—what are you doing ? Don't you know that you've grown up to be a woman since Jocelyn—Mr. Pierston—was last down here ? Of course you mustn't do now as you used to do three or four years ago ! ' "

When Jocelyn, who protests somewhat ineffectively that he expected the form of greeting he had received, has gone, her mother pursues her lecture on Avice's impropriety. The girl herself, with the simplicity of manners which runs like a thread through all this story of primitive Portland folk, who, till at all events comparatively recently, had several curious customs altogether out of keeping with the age in which they live, said simply enough, " I—I didn't think about how I was altered . . . . I used to kiss him, and he used to kiss me before he went away."

The girl goes out into the garden at the back of her mother's dwelling to expiate her impropriety, and to celebrate her newly acquired womanhood and grief with tears.

Jocelyn, not finding his father at home, also goes out into his garden, which abuts on that of the Caros. He hears Avice sobbing and moaning out " Oh, what shall I do, what *shall* I do ! . . . . So bold as it was—so shameless ! . . . . He will never forgive me—never, never like me again ! He'll think me a forward hussy . . ."

Jocelyn after hearing this retreats quickly as he can, but he is conscious that he is not displeased either by the girl's difficulty in seeing anything out of the way in her action, or by the fact that she is distressed lest she should by it have lost his good opinion.

But, with the difficulty he labours under all through his life, he is unable to feel that love has come, rather than the mere elusive fancy of the ideal, which already has on several occasions caused him trouble.

During the month of his holiday he sees much of Avice, and for a time is deluded into thinking that she is, after all, the " well-beloved " of his errant search.

The night before he is to leave again for London he has a tryst with Avice at King Henry Eighth's castle, which lies on a sandstone promontory almost straight across from the townlet of Portland on the mainland, north of which is Budmouth Regis (Weymouth). He is on his way thither when he is overtaken by a boy with a note. It is from Avice, who, doubtless from the newly awakened sense of the alteration which has taken place in them both since his last visit, declines to keep the tryst, saying, after an explanation which shows the subtility of the novelist's characterisation " On the whole, therefore, it is best that I should not come—if only for appearances—and meet you at the time and place suggesting " the custom," to others than ourselves, at least if known."

Church Hope Cove

Portland — "Isle of Slingers"

The " custom " referred to, it may be remarked, being one involving privileges as a rule coincident only with marriage, but given freely before the actual ceremony—till a comparatively recent period—by the primitive inhabitants of the Isle of Slingers.

One is left somewhat in doubt as to how much of this revolt against custom is caused by Avice's half-cultivated refinement, and how much by a latent fear that Jocelyn would despise her for yielding to it.

Jocelyn, disappointed at Avice's failure to meet him—not, however, angry with her ; which serves to show how fleeting and unsubstantial was her assumption of the role of the " well-beloved " in his eyes—goes on toward Budmouth.

While walking along the shore road he meets a woman almost overpowered by the wind, which has risen to the force of a gale. This woman, the daughter of a Mr. Bencomb, he assists. She is running away in a fit of anger at her father's treatment of her. Her destination is also London. They shelter for some hours under one of the lerrets (a large stoutly built boat), and then proceed to an hotel at Budmouth, and next morning to London.

Meanwhile, the " well-beloved " has assumed, with the rapidity which is so elusive and startling both to Jocelyn himself and to the reader, the form of this woman, Marcia Bencomb.

They live at a hötel together for some days while waiting to be married, and then eventually quarrel (before the ceremony can be performed) over their respective parents, and the merits of a feud which had existed for many years between them. They part ; and Jocelyn suffers from several incursions of the " well-beloved " into the temple he had prepared for *the* " well-beloved."

Twenty years pass, and he again finds himself in the " Isle of Slingers," present at the funeral of his Avice, who had married and left behind a daughter, also called Avice, who in time becomes another of the elusive visions of Jocelyn Pierston's " well-beloved."

This Ann Avice haunts him after his return to London, and he takes a lease of " Sylvania Castle," one of the few important residences on Portland, and settles there in the hope of his ideal ultimately materialising in the form of this second Avice.

Some of the finest pictures of local scenery and atmospheric conditions are found in this portion of the narrative. Avice the Second's temperament, Jocelyn discovers, is strangely affected by the weather. " Among other things," we are told, " he observed that she is often anxious when it rains. If, after a wet day, a golden streak appeared in the sky over Deadmen's Bay, under a lid of cloud (as it frequently does), her manner was joyous and her tread light."

Avice, at Jocelyn's behest, returns with him to London as a servant.

But the " well-beloved," in the case of Avice the Second, proves as elusive as that of Avice the First. And when Pierston confesses to the former that he was " the false young man " of whom her mother had spoken, she refuses to have anything more to do with him. Pressed for a reason why she will not accept his offer of marriage, she confesses that she is already married, having fallen a victim to the " island custom " the fear of which had probably lost Pierston to her mother as a husband.

This revelation causes the return of Avice and Pierston to Portland. After inspecting the register of marriages, and finding that Avice's story of marriage is true, Jocelyn leaves her.

Another twenty years passes, and the wanderer once more returns to his birthplace, having lived during the interval mostly in Rome and abroad. He finds Avice the Second a widow, and her daughter a young woman of about eighteen—a modernised and educated edition of her own mother and grandmother.

Avice the Third enters upon the scene of Pierston's life as her two former namesakes had done in the past.

Of this third incarnation Hardy says " He (Pierston) was subject to gigantic fantasies still. In spite of himself, the sight of the new moon, as representing one who, by her so-called inconstancy, acted up to his own idea of a migratory " Well-Beloved," made him feel as if his wraith, in a changed sex, had suddenly looked over the horizon at him."

In some respects the third Avice has more of her grandmother's temperament than of her mother's, for we are told that she possessed " the flippant, harmless freedom of the watering-place ' Miss ' " acquired during her life at a boarding school at Sandbourne (Bournemouth). Taught by past experiences, Jocelyn carefully guarded the secret that he had aforetime courted her mother and even grandmother !

" Like her granny, Avice was too inexperienced to be reserved," and the strange courtship, on account of this, proceeds apace. Pierston takes lodgings at Budmouth ; but finds many opportunities to come over to the island and take evening walks sometimes with Avice the third alone, sometimes with her mother as chaperone. With true Hardy selectiveness, Henry the Eighth's castle, which might have turned the course of events in her grandmother's day, is made the scene of Avice's enlightenment as regards Jocelyn's attentions.

In this castle, open to the sky, placed on the very verge of the rag-stone·cliff, Pierston consults with the mother as to her daughter's feelings, to discover that the former at least would not be averse to an alliance which had just eluded her and her mother before her.

Pierston somewhat neglects his courtship after this moonlight excursion, but returns to the island to bid Avice's mother good-bye, Mrs. Pierston, for such is her married name, is ill, and Avice the Third agrees, on her mother's representations, to marry Jocelyn.

After Mrs. Pierston's recovery she and Avice visit London; during which the final arrangements for the marriage are made. They then return to the island where Jocelyn was to follow them for the event. He does so in due course, only to find Mrs. Pierston again seriously ill, and while she lies a-bed, on what was to have been the wedding morn, Avice her daughter steals from the house in the company of a young Jersey man named Henri Leverre—the step-son of Marcia Bencomb, who had married his father. It was Marcia whose image had supplanted that of Avice the First for a brief period in Jocelyn Pierston's errant fancy.

Thus to some extent was justice done to the memory of that first Avice, whom Jocelyn had jilted.

Jocelyn in the end marries Marcia, but makes it perfectly plain to her that she is not, after all, the " well-beloved " of his life-long search. She marries him, apparently because she ought to have done so some forty years before.

Avice the Third, by this arrangement, becomes Pierston's daughter-in-law by marriage.

She is forgiven and provided with a house at Sandbourne, where she had secretly met her future husband while still a girl at the finishing school.

The novel thus ended is so unlike any other of the writer's works that it must be classed by itself as a more than slightly fantastic study of an unusual highly imaginative temperament.

The story probably interests the general reader chiefly because of its very elusiveness, and those who know " the Isle of Slingers " and its ways because of the fidelity of its descriptive passages. But it is one of the few novels of Hardy of which it is possible to give a synopsis without robbing the story of its chief charm.

*　　　*　　　*　　　*

THE MAYOR OF CASTERBRIDGE

The Mayor of Casterbridge competes with *Tess of the D'Urbervilles* in the centralisation of its interest and underlying drama. The scene of the story, too, is circumscribed, so that it is easy to follow and to identify many of its scenes. And the vivid characterisation; and, in some portions, suspense, adds materially to its interest. It may, also, be described as a biographical novel—the biography of its leading character, Michael Henchard, who became Mayor.

The scene, as a whole, is veritable and living Casterbridge, so accurately does Hardy describe the appearance of his native town; its life, as he knew it; and the characteristics of its inhabitants. Here and there the novelist has exercised—what he almost claims as his right—his disposition to move certain buildings and objects away from their actual sites. But this habit in the case of this story does not interfere with its interest; and sometimes, indeed, appears to add to its verisimilitude as a fitting background for the characters.

The opening scene of the story is at Weydon Priors, actually Weyhill. A little town, noted for centuries for its Autumn Fair, situated some four miles west of Andover and on the Wilts-Hampshire borderland.

Thus Hardy describes the scene " The spot stretched downwards into valleys and onward to other uplands dotted with " barrows," and trenched with the remains of prehistoric forts."

Though the Fair of late years has, as have many other events of a like nature, declined in importance it is still considered as the most important for sheep in the country. And is still worth visiting to meet with the rustic characters which still frequent it, and see the round-a-bouts, side-shows, wax works, fat ladies and thin gentlemen, thimble-riggers, swing boats and similar attractions. But Mrs. Goodenough, the seller of ' furmity,' compounded of corn in the grain, milk, raisins, currants and what not, will not be there to "lace" it with the rum that was Michel Henchard's undoing, nor would one, indeed, probably be able to get any 'furmity' today.

At Weydon Priors there are two double rows of permanent buildings, with brick or cob-walls, and with slate or galvanised iron roofs. And at fair times these are supplemented by the more usual caravans, tents, stalls and booths.

It was to this famous fair that Michael Henchard, his wife Susan, and their infant daughter Elizabeth-Jane came one night early in the story; and where Henchard, when drunk, sold his wife by auction to the highest bidder at five guineas. An event that was destined to lead to many complications.

The sailor, Richard Newson, who had bid, and produced the money, claimed his bargain.

Susan addressed her husband as follows, thinking the joke had gone far enough. "Now," said she "before you go further, Michael, listen to me. If you touch that money; I and this girl go with the man. Mind it is a joke no longer."

"A joke? Of course it is not a joke," shouted her husband . . . . I take the money; the sailor takes you. That's plain enough. It has been done elsewhere—and why not here?"

.   .   .   .

"Mike," she said, "I've lived with thee a couple of years, and had nothing but temper! Now I'm no more to 'ee; I'll try my luck elsewhere. 'Twill be better for me and the child, both. So good-bye!"

Next morning Henchard awoke in the booth where he had drunk the 'furmity.' He gradually recalled the events of the previous night, and he found his basket of tools near where he had fallen asleep on the grass. Among the odds and ends of rubbish thereby he saw a 'little shining object,' and picked it up. It was his wife's wedding ring!

The sailor's bank notes, the price he had received for Susan, he found in his pocket, and the scene came back to him.

Henchard then started off to walk to Casterbridge in a chastened mood. Regretting his folly and drunkenness. On his way he came to a village, and on seeing the church he entered it. Went up to the altar, and finding a book upon it he knelt down ; dropped his head upon the book, and solemnly vowed that he would avoid all strong drink for twenty years. Being a year for every one he had lived.

He then went on his way, enquiring here and there if anyone in the villages through which he passed had seen a sailor with a woman and little girl. He pursued his search for several days unsuccessfully. But his feeling of shame prevented him from widely advertising his loss.

Years passed and Henchard, who at Casterbridge had set up as a hay and corn dealer, prospered

The scene in time again changes back to Weydon Priors, into which village came a woman and a grown-up girl. Susan Henchard, now reputed to be a widow and Elizabeth-Jane. They ultimately made their way to the Fair ground. Susan found the old seller of ' furmity," Mrs. Goodenough, still carrying on her trade. She questioned her regarding her former visit when she had patronized her ' furmity,' and asked her whether she had since seen Henchard. The woman said that she had, and he had told her that should anyone enquire for him he lived at Castrbridge.

Susan at once decided to go there and try to find him.

Walking, and by lifts in waggons and carrier's carts, they at last came in sight of the town one evening as dusk was falling. On the summit of Mellstock Hill the two of them paused for a while.

Hardy describes the scene as follows : " The spot commanded a full view of the town and its environs," and he tells us that to Elizabeth-Jane it looked " an old-fashioned place, huddled all together ; and shut in by a square wall of trees, like a plot of garden ground by a box-edging."

Even today, from the vantage point they occupied, one gains a not dissimilar impression.

They went on and ultimately reached Casterbridge, and entering the town from the east they went up the High East Street. About half way they were attracted by a jollification at the King's Arms Hotel. In it Michael Henchard, now Mayor of the town, was entertaining a party of friends.

The striking bow-window of the room where the party had assembled is still to be seen, and one can imagine Susan and her grown-up daughter standing on the pavement across the road, and watching the passing of people crossing and re-crossing the window of the room.

Susan soon got in contact with her husband, Henchard, who received her kindly. The house where he lived was " one of the best, faced with red and grey old brick." The dwelling that Hardy may have had in mind is in South Street, set back a little from the roadway. Henchard had his barns and granaries on the slope of Durnover Hill at the back of the house.

The very night that Susan and her daughter reached Casterbridge there also arrived another traveller, a young Scot, Donald Farfrae by name, who was destined afterwards to play so important a part in the story. Becoming Henchard's head man, and ultimately his manager in his corn chandler's business ; and, after they had quarrelled, the cause of his financial ruin.

Henchard, it will be remembered, was at the time of Susan's reappearance engaged to Lucetta, a Miss Le Sueur, with whom he had met in Jersey. However, he was compelled to break off the engagement. And, having inherited a fortune through an aunt, Lucetta came to Casterbridge and lived at High Place Hall. Possibly Colliton House was in Hardy's mind, although the position, as described by him, is further in the direction of North Square. The bricked-up archway, with its mask above it, which Hardy describes as originally "exhibiting a comic leer . . . but generations of Caster-bridge boys had thrown stones at the mask, aiming at its open mouth, and the blows had chipped off the lips and jaws, as if they had been eaten away by disease," is to be seen in the Dorset County Museum.

Mixen Lane, which figures several times in the story, actually Mill Street, in the meadows of Fordington has been greatly altered by the passage of the years. Here, in the story, it is that one becomes acquainted with such shady characters as Mrs. Goodenough, the seller of ' furmity ' at the Weydon Priors Fair, Joshua Jopp, Mother Cuxson, Nance Mockridge, and other frequenters of the Peter's Finger Inn, in which the ' Skimmity ride ' was planned by Jopp and his associates, as a revenge upon Donald Farfrae when the latter married Lucetta Le Sueur. The Inn has been pulled down.

The ' Skimmington Ride ' was an ancient observance or custom designed to bring ridicule and discredit upon persons suspected or convicted of immorality, or even when convicted of being a quarrelsome couple ! The ' Ride ' consisted of making an effigy of the accused person, which was placed on a donkey, and escorted round the town by a procession of people dressed up and marching to discordant music. The effigy was in the end hung on a gallows and afterwards burned.

Lucetta Le Sueur, who had married Donald Farfrae, and whose illicit relations with Henchard had been found out by Jopp, who bore both Henchard and Farfrae grudges, and because of this sought to take revenge, was killed by the shock of her thus advertised disgrace, soon after the procession had passed beneath her windows.

Henchard lived for a time with Elizabeth-Jane, regarding her in the light of an adopted daughter, having learned that she was Newson's child, through a letter his wife, Susan, had left him when she died.

One of the ten oil paintings, by W. EMERSON BAUM,
from *Selected Short Stories of Thomas Hardy*

And here are

SELECTED SHORT STORIES
of THOMAS HARDY

Nine of the best and hardest-to-find Hardy stories illustrated with ten full color oil paintings by *W. Emerson Baum*. In keeping with the Hardy period, the binding is executed in two-color linen stamped with twenty-three carat gold; the edges are sprinkled in two colors. The text is printed in 12 point Baskerville type on ivory rag paper, with colored typographic decorations throughout.

WHIMSICAL TAL
of JERROLD

Anyone who has ever smile magazine *Punch* will be enc these fanciful satires, each illus lithograph crayon drawings *Daniel*. The book is bound in a printed, all-over pattern cloth spine panel stamped in twenty gold; edges are stained a rich br are not one, but *two* full color f reproduced from oil paintings. face is Dwiggins' Caledonia.

But when, after Lucetta's death Henchard learned that Farfrae and Elizabeth-Jane had agreed to marry, he went away from Casterbridge. One can follow him, a broken man, setting out one evening with his tool basket on his back, wearing his old working suit, with Elizabeth-Jane going with him as far as Grey's Bridge near the foot of High East Street.

Some little time afterwards hearing the date of Elizabeth-Jane's marriage he returned to Casterbridge to attend it. On his way, he paused, on the second night of his journey, at Shottsford Forum, where he bought a wedding present for Elizabeth-Jane in the shape of a goldfinch in a little cage.

He eventually reached Casterbridge, but too late to be at the wedding. From the top of Yalbury Hill, which runs down to the Fordington meadows and the approach to the town, he heard the " soft pealing of the Casterbridge bells, which was a signal that all had gone well " ; and that there had been no slip " twixt cup and lip in this case."

He reached the house of Donald Farfrae, and Elizabeth-Jane at last, to find dancing and other festivities taking place.

When he saw Elizabeth for a few moments she upbraids him for having told her real father, Captain Richard Newson, when the two had met some little time before, that she was dead.

Henchard attempted to defend himself for a moment, but abandoned the attempt because of the angry attitude of Elizabeth-Jane.

" Don't ye distress yourself on my account," he said, with a proud superiority, " I would not wish it—at such a time, too, as this. I have done wrong in coming to 'ee—I see my error. But it is only for once, so forgive it, I'll never trouble 'ee again, Elizabeth-Jane—no, not to my dying day. Good-bye ! Good-bye ! "

Both Elizabeth-Jane and Farfrae regretted what she had done and said to Henchard ; and the coldness of their parting.

They set out a month or so later to try and trace where he had gone. At last they got news when they were driving in Farfrae's gig along a country road and met a road-mender, who said he had seen ' such a man ' ; who had turned off the Salisbury coach road, at Weatherbury to " go along a forking highway which skirted the north of Egdon Heath." So Farfrae turned his horse's head in that direction.

But although they searched Egdon, which figures so prominently in several of the novels, far and wide, they found no trace of him they sought, till they met with a labourer, who had worked in Casterbridge and had become known to them.

' What Abel Whittle ; is it that ye are here ? ' said Farfrae.

' Ay, yes, sir. You see he was kind-like to mother when she were here below, though 'e was rough to me.'

' Who are you talking on ? '

' Oh, sir—Henchet. Didn't ye know it, ? He's just gone—about half-an-hour ago, by the sun ; for I've no watch to my name.'

' Not—dead ? ' faltered Elizabeth-Jane.

' Yes, ma'am, he's gone.'

And so on this tragic note ends *The Mayor of Casterbridge*, comparable with *Tess of the D'Urbervilles* in the depth and inevitableness of its tragedy.

More than, perhaps, in any other of Hardy's novels is it possible in this one to trace and follow up the movements of the characters and the scenic environment of the story. For so much of the latter survives unaltered or only comparatively slightly so.

*   *   *   *

UNDER THE GREENWOOD TREE

Under the Greenwood Tree, The second of the novels to attain publication, attracted considerable attention at the time, and was recognized by competent critics as work of a promising character by a new writer of individuality.

It is concerned with the rural life of Wessex that is today almost non-existent in the form in which Hardy depicts it. It is, therefore, of value as a first-hand record of habits, practices and customs that were still existent in Wessex in the early part and middle half of the last century.

Then, the music to lead the singing at services in many churches was provided by a village orchestra, usually occupying a gallery, as was the case at Puddletown and Stinsford Churches. Antiquarians and music lovers and students will be interested to learn that " Their music in those, now seemingly so far off times, was performed from MSS written by the performers themselves. These were copied in the evenings after the day's work was done ; and the music books were usually home-made and home bound."

Here and there examples have been preserved, and are treasured by the families, which in their great grandfather's day, provided the instrumentalists for Sunday and other services. It is recorded, too, that some of the instruments themselves were made by the players.

Occasionally one still comes across examples of both music and instruments in museums, and family's of the old tradition.

As for the music it was of wider scope than the fact that its prime object was to lead the singing on Sunday morning and other services would suggest. Not only did it comprise hymn tunes that were well-known and some of them very ancient ; but also carols, secular songs, metrical psalm tunes, and those of country dances, and of the customary songs sung at festal gatherings.

It will be remembered by readers of Hardy's Life that the novel under consideration originally bore the title of *Under the Greenwood Tree or The Mellstock Quire*, and this accounts for the prominent part in the story devoted to village choir music. The spelling as used by Hardy was the common one for ' choir ' down to the commencement of the eighteenth century ; and, indeed, prevailed in Wessex until a considerably later time. So important were the frequent services of the instrumentalists in the choirs of the churches, that they figure not only prominently in this novel, but in several of Hardy's poems. Notably in *The Dead Quire, The Noble Lady's Tale*, and *The Rash Bride.*

Unfortunately today, owing to many buildings having been pulled down since the date of this story, round about 1840, one is generally speaking only able to trace the localities of the scenes depicted, rather than certain buildings also. For example the term Mellstock included several isolated buildings in Stinsford ; the two Bockhamptons, Bhompston, Higher Kingston, Kingston Maurward, with Stinsford House. All of which may be considered as comprised in the general scene of the story.

Under the Greenwood Tree deals with the pastoral courtship of Dick Dewy and Fancy Day, and early in the story, one meets with the famous Mellstock Quire in Mellstock Lane. It is on its way to Dick Dewy's home at Upper Mellstock, easily identified with Upper Bockhampton. Fancy Day, who, for those times had been well-educated, was the schoolmistress at the Church School at Lower Mellstock, which may be taken as Lower Bockhampton, where there is a school today that may be that which Hardy had in mind.

The Mellstock Quire folk were thirsty souls, and so they visited, the evening on which we make their acquaintance in the story, several houses of friends for refreshment. And that of Farmer Shiner, who also was in love with Fancy Day, and whose suit was favoured by her father owing to Shiner's substantial position.

This story has more humour to the page in the early and later portions than is to be found in any of Hardy's other novels, for our author has grouped a wonderful selection of typical country characters together, William Dewy, grandfather of Dick, his father Reuben, Mr. Penny, Mr. Spinks, Fancy Day, described by Mr. Penny, one of the musicians, as " nate a little figure of fun as ever I see, and just husband-high." Michael and Reuben Mail, who were the tenor and second violins, Mrs. Dewy, Billy Chimlen, Bowman, and Farmer Fred Shiner. The scene of the Christmas Eve carolling, and that of the Quire's wanderings from house to house, " imbibing liquid refreshment" as they go, has the true Hardy touch.

Especially the scene outside the Schoolhouse, where Fancy Day, lived, and later at the Vicarage, where the Rev. Arthur Maybold, was aroused from his slumbers by the serenading of his parishioners.

The scene of the Christmas Day service in the Mellstock (Stinsford) Church, and the party afterwards in the evening at Reuben Dewys' house are very vividly described, and amusing.

How far we have changed from that time is shown by the check then put on the junior members of the party who were longing to dance. Mrs. Penny remarks " If you have a party on Christmas-day-night, 'tis only fair and honourable to the Church of England to have it a sit-still party. Jigging parties be all very well, and this, that and therefore ; but a jigging party looks suspicious. O, yes ; stop till the clock strikes young folk—so says I. And Christmas Day is over."

It happened that some warm mead accidentally got into Mr. Spink's head about this time.

" Dancing," he said, " is a most strengthening, enlivening, and courting movement, especially with a little beverage added."

But no dancing was allowed until the clock struck twelve, for which the younger members had watched anxiously.

Hardy embroiders the festive scene with what are actual memories of his youth.

The fun, especially in " that most delightful of country dances, beginning with six-hand-round," became fast and furious. Young Dick secured Fancy Day for a partner ; and his father, Reuben, became so heated with the exertion that he proposed that the men should take off their coats. His wife said " such low notions you have Reuben. Nothing but strip will go down with you, when you are a-dancing. Such a hot man as he is."

Unfortunately, in Stinsford Church time has caused changes to be made. It has been restored or repaired twice in the last half-century, and with the restorations the ancient musicians' gallery, which plays so important a part in the story has been removed. But the Church still contains some interesting monuments to the Pitt family : and also a brass tablet recording members of Hardy's family who lie buried here. The enormous vases, capping the pillars of the entrance gate to the churchyard, described by Hardy, still exist.

Geoffrey, Fancy Day's father was the keeper of Yalbury Great Wood, actually Yellowham Wood. And this more eternal feature of the scene of the story remains as it was when Dick Dewy made his way with " Smart the mare and the light spring-cart " to fetch Nancy Day, who had been appointed to the Church School at Mellstock, and to take her to her new home. The keeper's cottage, though somewhat altered from Hardy's description, still stands a little way off the road, and is to be reached by a drive at the bottom of the hill between Dorchester and Puddletown.

Fancy Day was loved not only by Dick Dewy and Farmer Shiner, but also by the Vicar, the Rev. Arthur Maybold. While engaged to Dick Dewy she did not tell the Vicar of the fact ; who proposed to her and was accepted, as she was dazzled by the prospect, and, from the fact that she was a well-educated girl, was attracted to him.

The Vicar soon afterwards met Dick as they were both on their way to Casterbridge, Dick told the Vicar that he was engaged to Fancy, and the astonished man, when they parted at almost the foot of High East Street, leant over the parapet of the bridge spanning the river, to think over the matter. Seeing " without heeding—how the water came rapidly from beneath the arches, glided down a little steep and then spread itself over a pool . . . . "

On his return to the Vicarage he wrote to Fancy and told her what had happened. Adding " Will you in justice to an honest man, who relies upon your word to him, consider whether, under the circumstances, you can honourably forsake him."

After he had written the letter, and sent it to Fancy by a boy, another came with a letter from Fancy Day asking him to " generously allow me to withdraw the answer too hastily given." Her acceptance of his proposal of marriage.

The story which is a rather ' thin ' one, ends happily with the boisterous rustic wedding of Dick Dewy and Fancy Day, with its procession to the Church among " the dark perpendicular firs, like shafted columns of a cathedral, now under the broad beeches in bright young leaves ; then through a hazel copse, matted with primroses and wild hyacinths, into the high road. Every man to his maid."

And after the ceremony, to a gathering of many relatives and friends, old and young, at the bride's home, with dancing on the greensward.

*   *   *   *

This novel, that may be justly called one chiefly of character and environment, covers a fairly wide area of country, including Minterne Magna, Melbury Sampford, Melbury Osmund, Sherborne, Milton Abbey, Blandford Forum, and Weymouth.

Though not one of Hardy's best stories it is distinguished by the interest of the characters depicted, and the attractiveness of the scenery amid which they pass their lives.

The story is indeed rather ' over-plotted,' if one may use such a term, but some of the rural scenes and descriptions are excellent. Among the leading characters is George Melbury, and here one has a Hardy liking occasionally to give a character a part of the name of a village or place, there are two villages in this novel with the name of Melbury, just as in *Jude the Obscure* one has the great-aunt of Jude, named Miss Drusilla Fawley, and one of the villages appearing in the story is named Fawley Magna.

George Melbury, a timber merchant, early in the story is contemplating marrying his daughter to Giles Winterborne, engaged in the apple trade, and cider making at the various farms. Melbury had apparently decided to take this step as a sort of reparation for having cheated a friend of boyhood's days, John Winterborne, the father of Giles, out of the girl to whom he was engaged, and by marrying her.

Grace Melbury had been unusually well-educated for her station, and because of her lady-like manners, and good education became acquainted with a Mrs. Felice Charmond, and also with a Dr. Fitzpiers. Grace fell in love with the latter and married him. Mrs. Charmond was a rich woman, living at Hintock House, who also fell in love with the doctor, who, though married to Grace returned her affection, and eventually they ran away together to the Continent. They, however, quarrelled and parted. Soon afterwards Felice Charmond was shot by an American, whose proposal to marry her she had rejected.

Meanwhile, after Mrs. Charmond and Dr. Fitzpiers had gone away together, George Melbury heard that a new divorce law had come into operation, and tried to get a divorce from Fitzpiers for his daughter Grace, but failed to do so. Then news came that Dr. Fitzpiers had parted from Mrs. Charmond, and was on his way back to England.

Grace decided that she would not meet or see him, and one day hearing he was on his way to see her she left home to go and visit a friend. She was overtaken by a storm, and took refuge in a hut occupied by Giles Winterborne, who was taken seriously ill. Grace found Giles unconscious, and sent for Dr. Fitzpiers to come and see him. He came, but Giles died.

Then Grace returned to live with her father for a time, and Fitzpiers left the neighbourhood, and went as an assistant to another doctor in the Midlands.

After a time his love for Grace revived and he tried to get her to forgive him, and come to live with him. He visited her often. And a man named Tim Tangs, a wood-cutter, whose wife formerly had been seduced by Fitzpiers seeing the latter often in the neighbourhood when he was visiting Grace, thought wrongly that Fitzpiers came to see his wife to pester her again. To take his revenge he set a man trap in the path the doctor always followed. It was, however, Grace who fell the victim of his plot, for she trod on the trap on her way to meet Fitzpiers, and although not seriously injured had her clothing very much torn, and hid behind a hedge to make what repairs she could. Fitzpiers came along on his way to meet Grace, as usual, and, seeing who it was she came out and told him what had happened.

Very much alarmed and upset at what had happened, he asked her again to forgive him. He was staying in the neighbourhood at the time at an hotel, and Grace, relenting, went away with him and stayed at the hotel. When her father and neighbours, alarmed at Grace's disappearance, at last tracked her to the hotel at Sherton Abbas, she refused to go back with her father.

The story at times lags, but the rural characters and scenes are described admirably, and there is a remarkably appealing character, Marty South, in love with Giles Winterborne, that takes hold of the reader, though she only plays a small part in the story.

And so the end.

LOCALITIES OF THE NOVELS

NOTE.—The names given are those of Hardy, which may be identified with the actual places by reference to the Topographical Indices.

"A LAODICEAN"
(1881)
The chief scenes of this novel are set at Stancy Castle, Somerset, near Minehead, Markton, and others in London.

"A PAIR OF BLUE EYES"
(1873)
The chief scenes of this novel are set at Endelstow, near Boscastle, Plymouth, St. Launce's, in London and on the Continent.

"DESPERATE REMEDIES"
(1871)
The chief scenes are set at Knapwater House near Casterbridge, Budmouth, Southampton, London, Casterbridge, also in the village of Tolchurch.

"FAR FROM THE MADDING CROWD"
(1874)
The scenes of this novel are set in Weatherbury, Casterbridge and Norcombe, between Dorchester and Bridport.

"JUDE THE OBSCURE"
(1895)
The scenes of this novel are set in a wide area, and include Marygreen, Christminster, Shaston, Melchester, Aldbrickham and Kennetbridge.

"TESS OF THE D'URBERVILLES"
(1891)
The scenes of this novel are set in Shaston, Marlott, the Blackmoor Vale, Kingsbere, Sherton Abbas, Stourcastle, Talbothays, The Chase, Trantridge, Wellbridge, Sandbourne, Wintoncester.

"THE HAND OF ETHELBERTA"
(1876)
The scenes of this novel are set in London, Anglebury, Knollsea, Sandbourne, Melchester and Enkworth.

"THE MAYOR OF CASTERBRIDGE"
(1886)
The story opens at Weydon Priors, but all the principal scenes are set in Casterbridge.

"THE RETURN OF THE NATIVE"
(1878)
The chief scenes of this story are set on Egdon Heath.

" THE TRUMPET MAJOR " . . (1880)	The scenes of this novel are set in the vicinity of Budmouth, Overcombe and the Isle of Slingers, with mentions of Anglebury, Wetherbury, and Casterbridge.
" THE WELL-BELOVED " . . (1897)	The scenes of this novel are chiefly set in the Isle of Slingers and London.
" TWO ON A TOWER " . . . (1882)	The scenes of this novel are chiefly set in Welland, with some at Bath and Melchester.
" UNDER THE GREENWOOD TREE " . (1872)	The scenes of this novel are set in Mellstock and Casterbridge.
" THE WOODLANDERS " . . (1887)	The scenes of this novel are chiefly set in the Hintocks, Sherton Abbas, Middleton Abbey, Shottsford Forum, Budmouth, etc.

TOPOGRAPHICAL INDEX (A)

Note.—The places and buildings included in this Index comprise only those contained in the text of the book ; and in the novels and poems, the scenes of which are referred to or described in the area which can most truly be considered as constituting Hardy's Wessex.

The identification of the places was made possible by visits to them paid by the present writer, often in company with Mr. Hardy himself ; and by means of a list kindly supplied in his own handwriting. In the covering letter he mentioned that he had frequently only used portions of a scene, excluding unessentials ; also had transferred buildings and other objects from their actual sites to others he thought fitted in with more distinction as he imagined the scene. Also, in several instances, the characteristics of two or more buildings may have been combined for the purposes of the story.

This explanation of transposition will serve to account for any possible discrepancies that appear to have occurred. Indeed, the identification in some instances can only be deemed approximate.

Actual Names.	*Hardy Names.*
Affpuddle	*East Egdon.*
Beaminster	*Emminster.*
Bere Regis	*King's Bere.*
Blandford Forum	*Shottsford Forum.*
Bournemouth	*Sandbourne.*
Bridport	*Port Bredy.*
Canford Manor	*Chene Manor, also Aldbrickham.*
Cerne Abbas	*Abbot's Cernal.*
Charborough (nr. Wimborne)	*Welland House.*
Cranborne Chase	*Chase (The).*
Cranborne	*Chasetown or Chaseborough.*
Dole's Ash (nr. Puddletrenthide)	*Flintcomb Ash.*
Dorchester	*Casterbridge.*
Dunster	*Markton.*
Dunster Castle	*Stancy Castle.*
East Stoke	*Holmstoke.*
Eggardon Hill	*Norcombe.*
Encombe	*Enkworth.*
Evershot	*Evershead.*
Farrs (nr. Pamphill)	*Yewsholt Lodge.*
Fordington	*Durnover.*
Fortune's Well (Portland)	*Street of Wells (The).*
Gillingham	*Leddenton.*
Hazelbury Bryan	*Nuzzlebury.*
Horton Inn	*Lornton Inn.*
Jordon Hill (nr. Weymouth)	*Clavinium.*
Kingston House (nr. Stinsford)	*Knapwater House.*
Lulworth	*Lulstead.*
Maiden Newton	*Chalk Newton.*
Marnhull	*Marlott.*
Melbury Osmund	*Little Hintock.*

Actual Names.	*Hardy Names.*
Melbury Sampford	*King's Hintock Court.*
Milborne St. Andrew's	*Millpond St. Jude's.*
Milton Abbey	*Middleton Abbey.*
Norris Hill Farm (between Stinsford and Tincleton)	*Talbothays.*
Okeford Fitzpaine	*Oakbury Fitzpiers.*
Oxford	*Christminster.*
Owermoigne	*Nether Moynton.*
Pennsylvania Castle (Portland)	*Sylvania Castle.*
Poole	*Havenpool.*
Portesham	*Po'sham.*
Portland	*Isle of Slingers (The).*
Puddlehinton and Puddletrenthide	*Longpuddle.*
Puddletown	*Weatherbury.*
Poundbury Camp (Dorchester)	*Poundbury, or Pummerie.*
Ringstead (nr. Lulworth Cove)	*Ringsworth.*
Sandsfoot Castle (nr. Weymouth)	*Henry VIII Castle.*
Shaftesbury	*Shaston.*
Sherborne	*Sherton Abbas.*
St. Alban's Head	*St. Aldhelm's Heart.*
Sturminster Newton	*Stourcastle.*
Sutton Poyntz	*Overcombe.*
Stinsford (and adjacent hamlets)	*Mellstock.*
Swanage	*Knollsea.*
Tincleton	*Stickleford.*
Tolpuddle	*Tolchurch.*
Troy Town (nr. Puddletown)	*Roy Town.*
Turnworth	*Great Hintock House.*
Wareham	*Anglebury, also Southerton.*
Weymouth	*Budmouth.*
Wimborne	*Warborne.*
Winchester	*Wintoncester.*
Green Hill (nr. Bere Regis)	*Woodbury Hill.*
Wool	*Wellbridge.*
Yellowham Wood (between Dorchester and Puddletown)	*Yalbury Wood.*

TOPOGRAPHICAL INDEX (B)

Hardy Names.	*Actual Names.*
Abbot's Cernel	Cerne Abbas.
Anglebury, also Southerton	Wareham.
Bindon Abbey	at Wool.
Emminster	Beaminster.
Buckbury Fitzpiers	Okeford Fitzpaine.
Budmouth	Weymouth.
Casterbridge	Dorchester.
Chalk Newton	Maiden Newton.
Chase (The)	Cranborne Chase.
Chene Manor	Canford Manor.
Christminster	Oxford.
Corvsgate	Corfe.
Corvsgate Castle	Corfe Castle.
Clavinium	Jordan Hill (nr. Weymouth).
Dairies (Valley of the Great)	Vale of the Frome or Var.
Dairies (Valley of the Little)	Blackmoor Vale.
Durnover	Fordington.
East Egdon	Affpuddle.
East Quarriers	Easton (Portland).
Egdon Heath	Heath between Wareham and Dorchester.
Emminster	Beaminster.
Endelstom	St. Juliot's.
Enkworth	Encombe (nr. Swanage).
Evershed	Evershot.
Flintcomb Ash	Dole's Ash (nr. Puddletown).
Flytchett	Lytchett (nr. Poole).
Great Hintock	Minterne Magna.
Greenhill	Woodbury Hill (nr. Bere Regis).
Henry VIII Castle	Sandsfoot Castle.
Haggardon Hill (nr. Bridport)	Eggardon Hill (nr. Bridport).
Havenpool	Poole.
Holmstoke	East Stoke and Holme.
Hope Church	Church Hope, Portland.
Isle of Slingers	Portland.
Ivelchester	Ilchester.
King's Bere	Bere Regis.
King's Hintock	Melbury Sampford.
King's Hintock Court	Melbury Park.
Knollsea	Swanage.
Leddenton	Gillingham.
Lewgate	Lewstock.
Little Hintock	Melbury Osmund.
Longpuddle, Lower	Puddlehinton.
Longpuddle, Upper	Puddletrenthide.
Lornton Inn	Horton Inn.
Lulstead Cove	Lulworth Cove.
Marlott	Marnhull.
Markton	Dunster

INDEX

THE NOVELS